BO DOG

The way I see it, Stuff Happens...

(A Collection of Cartoons by Ron Lukesh & BO)

CARTOON BOOK FOR DOG LOVERS

Field Mouse BOOKS™
P.O. Box 392 - G.I. NE 68802-0392

No part of this publication may be reproduced, stored, or transmitted in any form, or by any means, anywhere in the world, without the permission in writing from the artist and/or publisher.

Cartoons and book copyright ©2013 Ronald E. Lukesh
All rights reserved. Cartoons copyright ©2000, 2012, 2013
Published by Field Mouse Productions
Grand Island and Palmer, Nebraska, USA
www.fieldmousebooks.com
www.fieldmouseproductions.com
Book first printed, 2013
Printed in the United States of America
R.L.: All ages   I.L.: All ages

Lukesh, Ronald E., 1948-
Bo Dog: The Way I See It, Stuff Happens
SUMMARY: A humorous collection of seasonal and other cartoons drawn straight from the mind and actions of Bo, a real American Eskimo Dog. A cartoon book for dog lovers of all ages. (Cartoons compiled and reprinted from those previously drawn and syndicated in newspapers by the artist.)
1. Dogs—Cartoons. 2. Pets—Cartoons. 3. Animals—Cartoons. 4. Cartoons and caricatures. 5. Comic books, strips, etc. 6. Wit and humor.
I. Title. II. Subtitle. III. It's a Dog's Life!
Illus. Ron Lukesh (Ronald E. Lukesh)
741.5 [E] [808.7] [636.7]   ISBN 978-0-9647586-7-4

This book is dedicated to Dog Lovers and Animal Lovers, Pet Rescue Shelters, Equine Rescue Ranches, local Humane Societies, and caring Veterinarians and staff everywhere, and to our good friends: Tim and Louise Mohanna, Roger Welsch who gave us an autographed copy of his wonderful book *Life With Dogs* when Bo was literally on his last legs, Roger's wife Linda (who appreciates a good dog cartoon), neighbors Dan and Cheryl Placzek who owned Caramel (Bo's "dream girl" Golden Lab who lived across the alley), Kristen Friesen who put Bo's picture in *Nebraska Life Magazine*, the very caring staff at Dr. Melissa (Missy) Girard-Lemon's Animal Medical Clinic in Grand Island, former veterinarians Dr. Dick Wampler and Dr. Bill and Mary Ann Carson, our UPS delivery man Bruce, our grandnephew Colby and his sisters (Brit and Kenzee) who were so wonderfully patient with Bo, and Bo's new rescue dog/foster brother Jasper who wants (and is giving inspiration for) his own cartoon book.
But most of all, this book is dedicated with love,
to the memory of the late great Bo
(aka Bo Dog, or Boo, or Boo Boo,
or The Boogie Woogie Boo Boo Boy)
who shared his life with us for 15 years
and who is still with us in spirit and in these cartoons.

This photo is the only remaining picture taken of Bo the day he came to live with us. The photo quality is not good, but he was so cute!

Bo, late in life, with his good friends Brit, Kenzee, and Colby

Foreword–

Bo came to live with us the day before Thanksgiving, 1995. We could see from day one that he was going to be a character. I had taken off my shoes and set them next to the chair. I looked down and little Bo was resting on the top of my shoes, much like little puppies in a pile when they are all together.

At first I would tell Jean, my wife who was also a school teacher, about the funny things he did. Most of the time it was to amuse himself, but often times he did things to amuse me. So, I started drawing little cartoons about those things for Jean too.

In the months and years that followed I had collected several cartoons. A good friend of mine owned a weekly newspaper and print shop. Our friend Tim and I decided we should share the single frame cartoons with other dog owners. The series was aptly named, BO DOG.

Bo was with us for fifteen years. He was a joy to have as a friend and companion. If he were here today, he'd probably have something special to say to me as I write this.

We missed our Bo Dog so much that Jean went looking for another American Eskimo dog and found just the right one in a rescue center. We think he had been a companion for two little girls and their mother and they were moving, and could no longer keep him. We drove 300 miles to get him and bring him home with us. Jasper, as they had named him, continually reminds us of his look-alike foster brother Bo even though Jasper has a different personality. He continues to give us the joys of living together as a family. So here is a compilation of Bo events, views of his joys, desires, and sometimes his short comings, and reminders of his wonderful life with us.

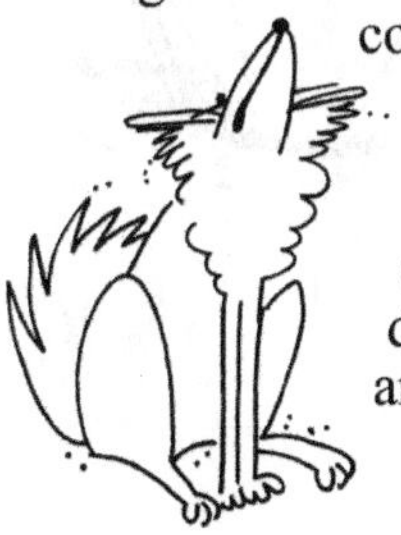

–Designer-Illustrator, Ronald E. Lukesh.

Table of Contents

Winter

Spring

Summer

Fall

© 2000, 2012 RON LUKESH

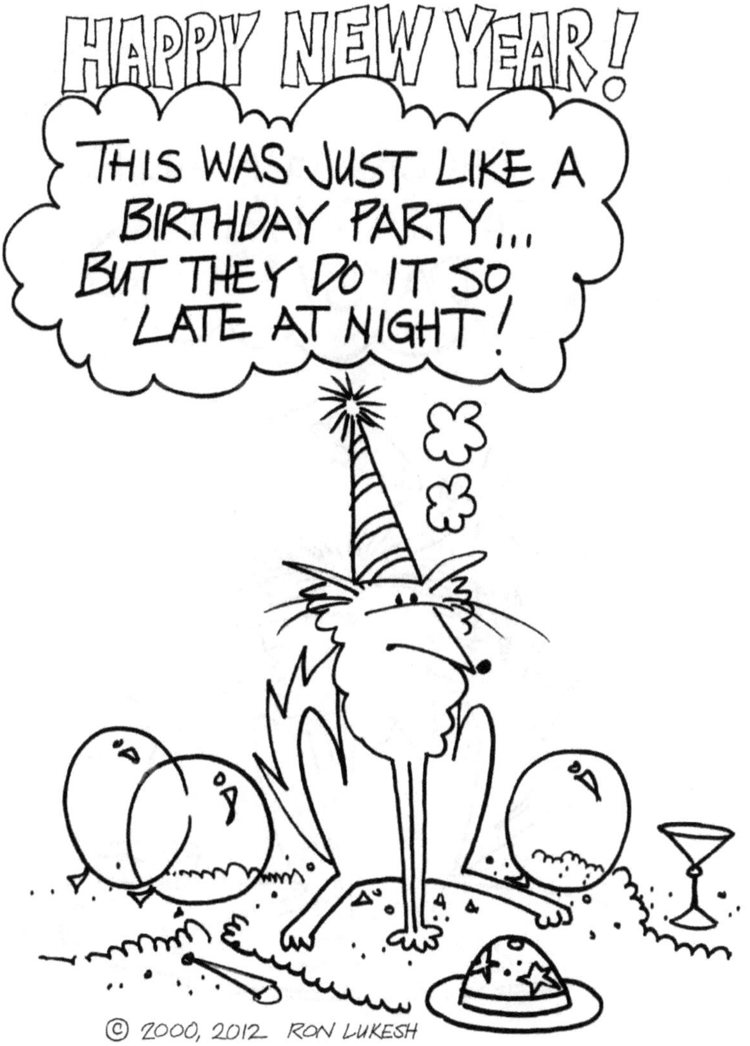
HAPPY NEW YEAR!
THIS WAS JUST LIKE A BIRTHDAY PARTY... BUT THEY DO IT SO LATE AT NIGHT!
© 2000, 2012 RON LUKESH

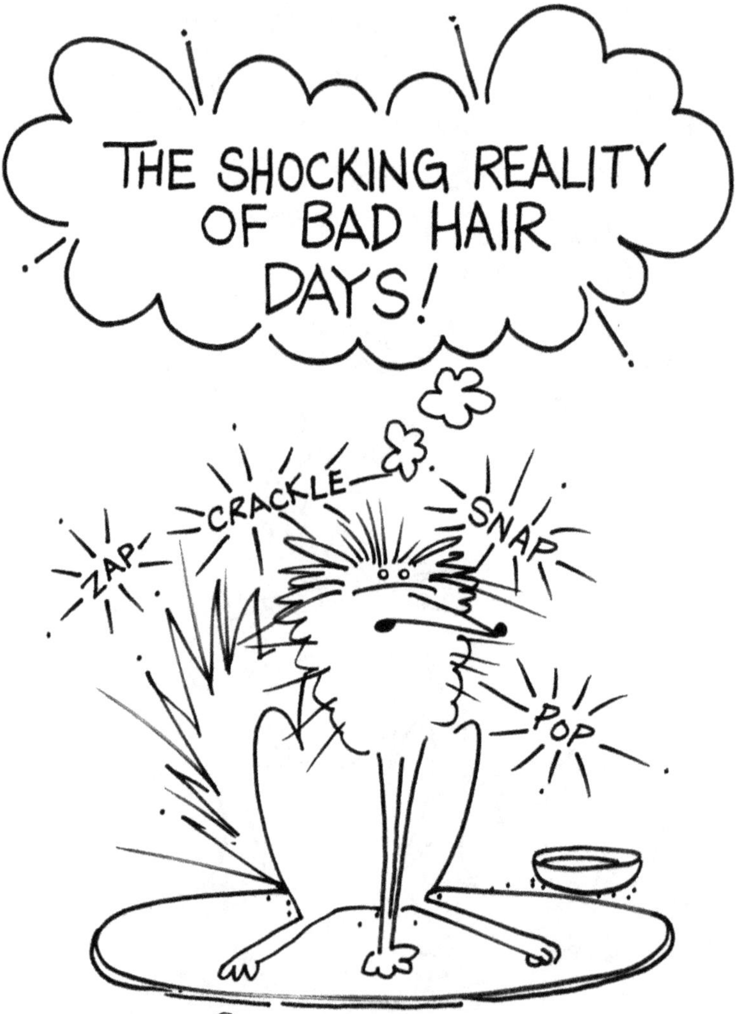
THE SHOCKING REALITY OF BAD HAIR DAYS!
ZAP
CRACKLE
SNAP
POP

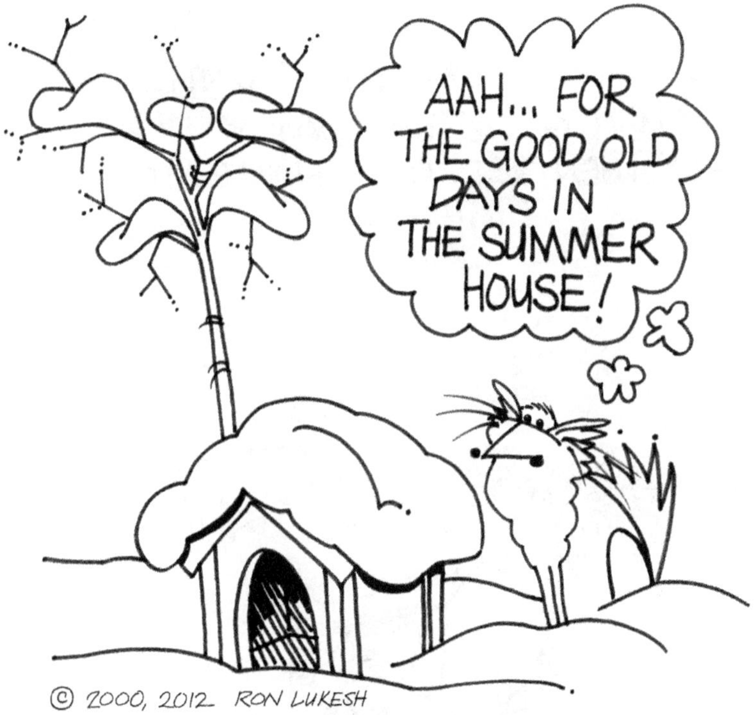
AAH... FOR THE GOOD OLD DAYS IN THE SUMMER HOUSE!
© 2000, 2012 RON LUKESH

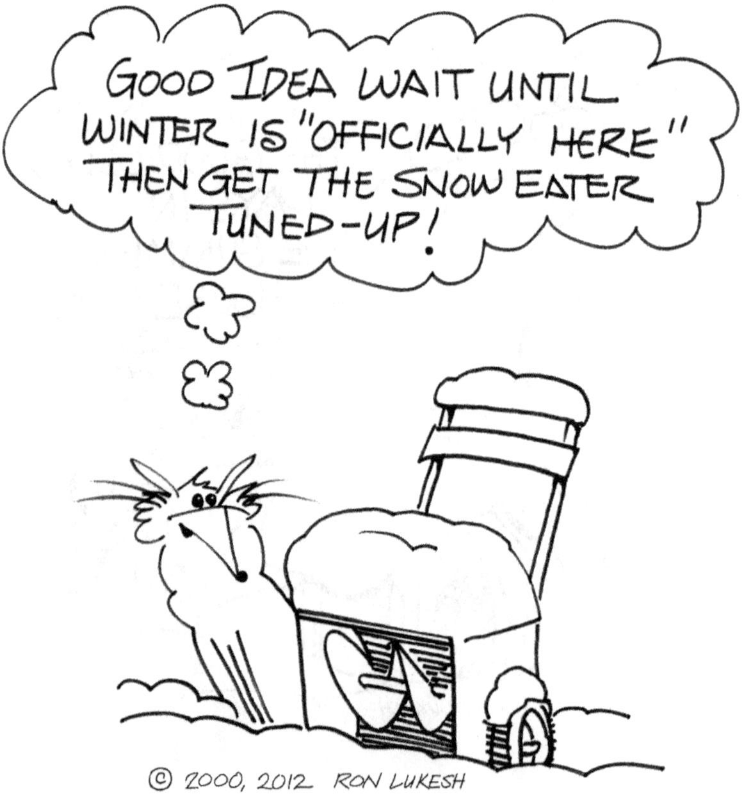
GOOD IDEA WAIT UNTIL WINTER IS "OFFICIALLY HERE" THEN GET THE SNOW EATER TUNED-UP!
© 2000, 2012 RON LUKESH

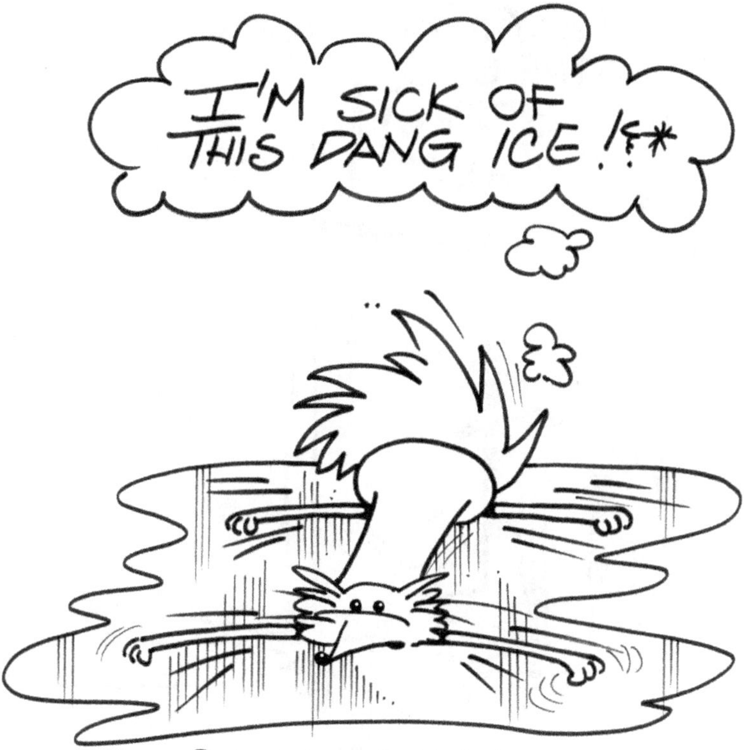
I'M SICK OF
THIS DANG ICE !?*

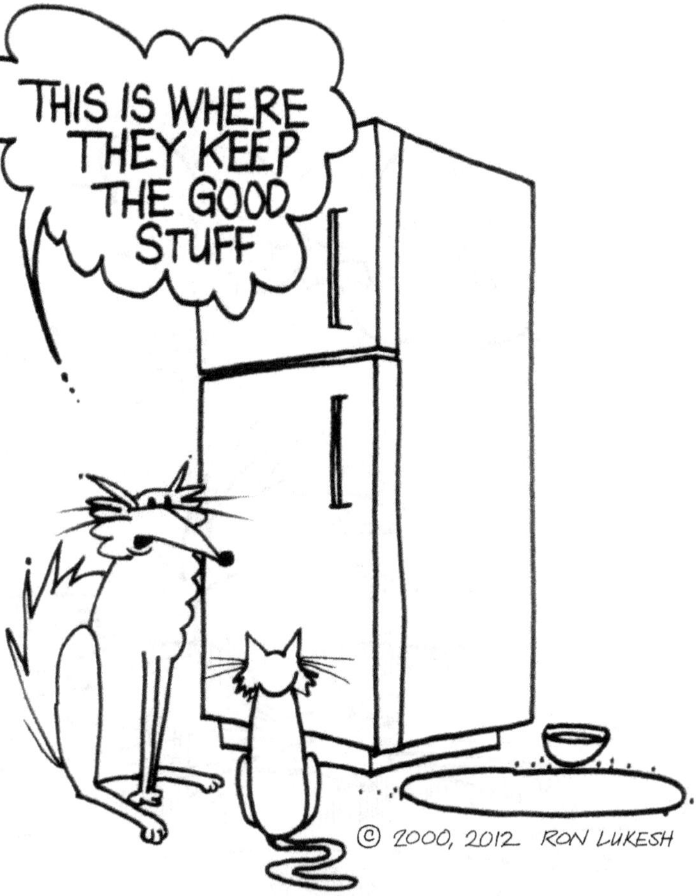
THIS IS WHERE THEY KEEP THE GOOD STUFF
© 2000, 2012 RON LUKESH

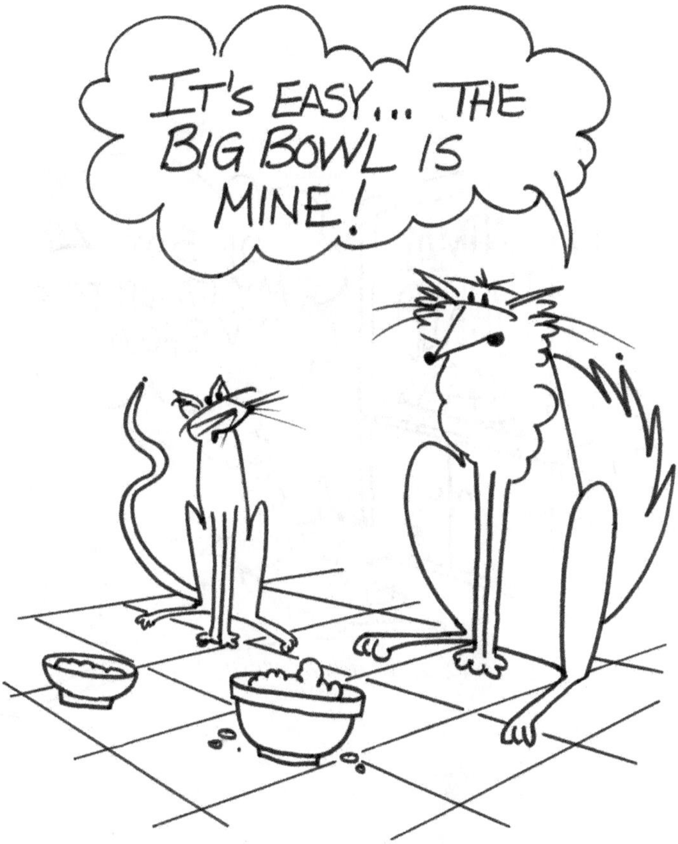
IT'S EASY... THE BIG BOWL IS MINE!

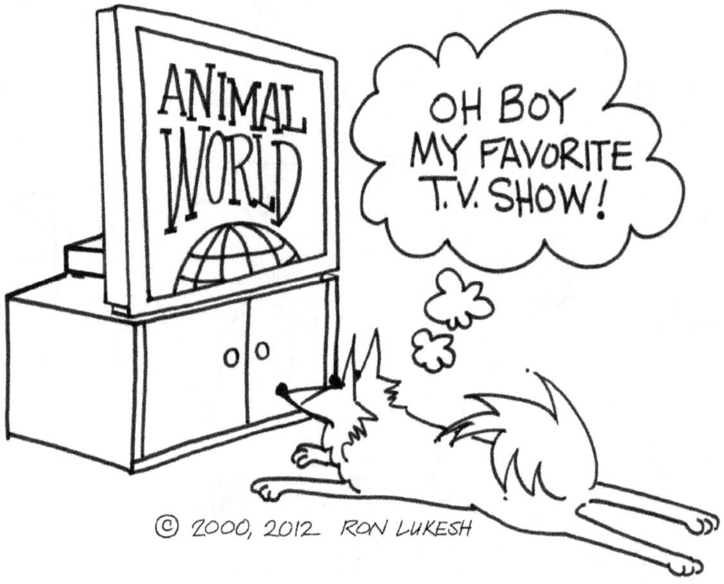
ANIMAL WORLD
OH BOY MY FAVORITE T.V. SHOW!
© 2000, 2012 RON LUKESH

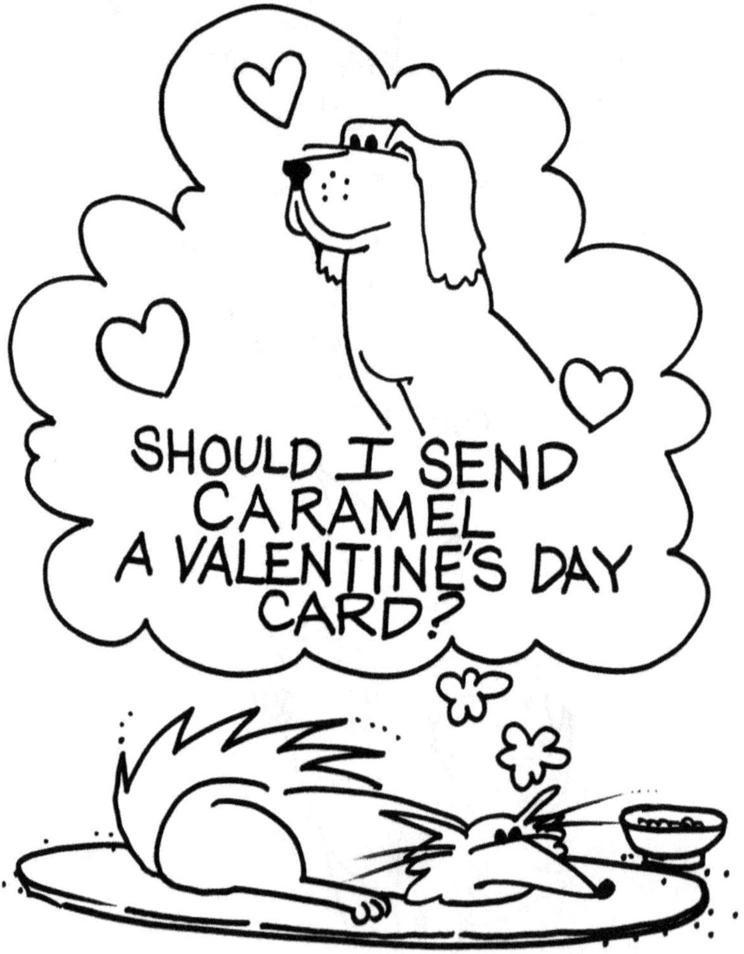
SHOULD I SEND CARAMEL A VALENTINE'S DAY CARD?

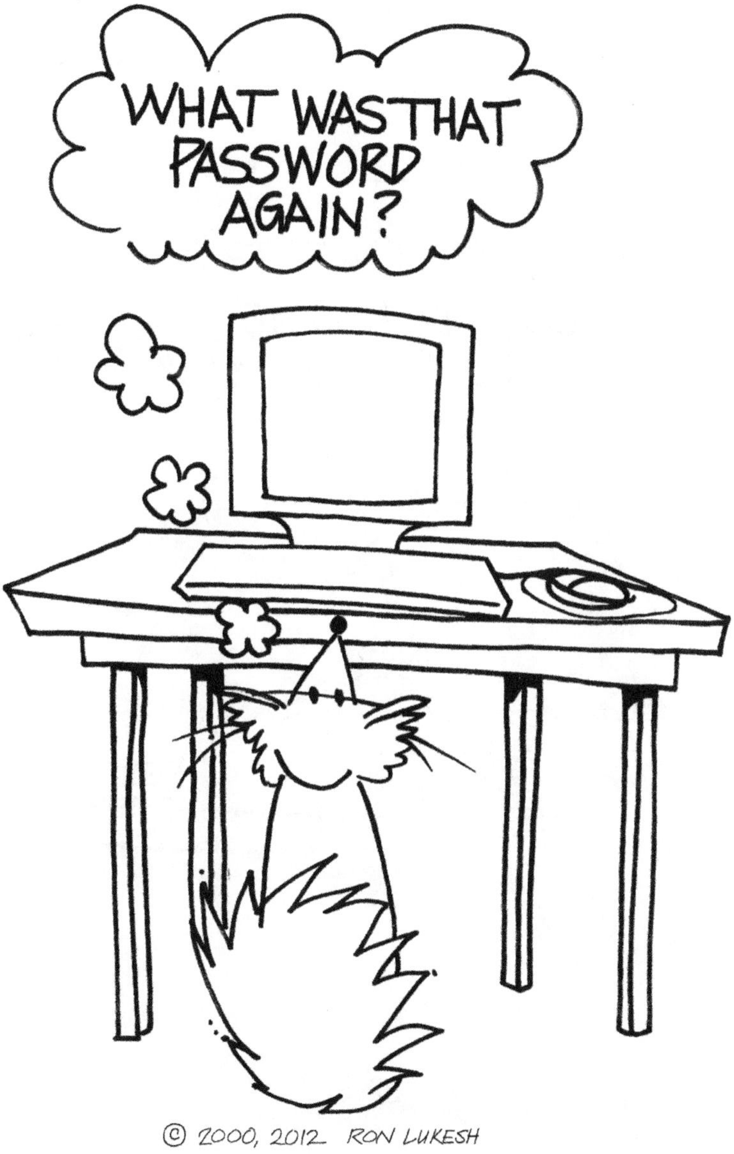
WHAT WAS THAT PASSWORD AGAIN?

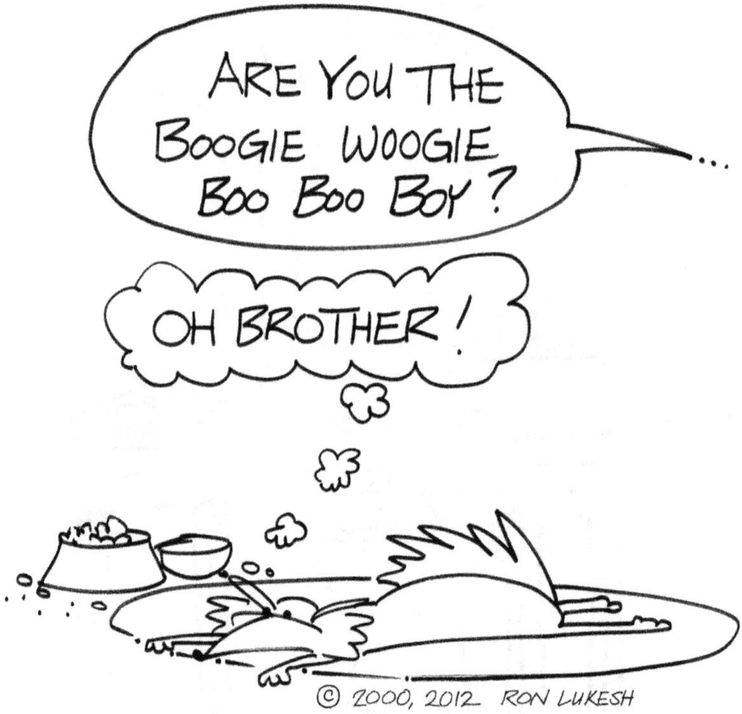
ARE YOU THE BOOGIE WOOGIE BOO BOO BOY?
OH BROTHER!
© 2000, 2012 RON LUKESH

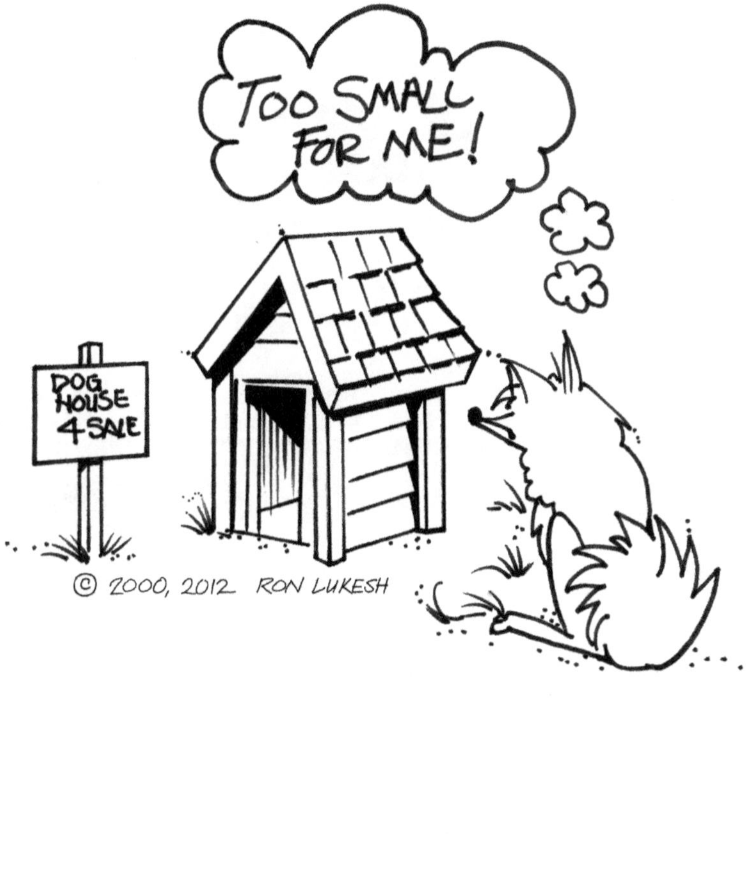
TOO SMALL FOR ME!
DOG HOUSE 4 SALE
© 2000, 2012 RON LUKESH

Spring

© 2000, 2012 RON LUKESH

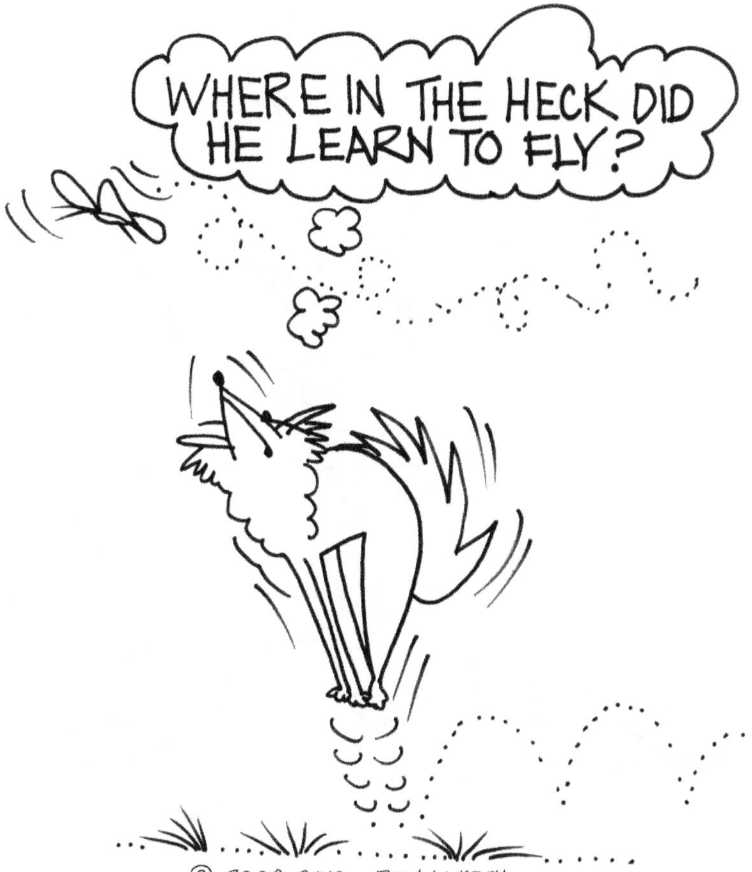
WHERE IN THE HECK DID HE LEARN TO FLY?

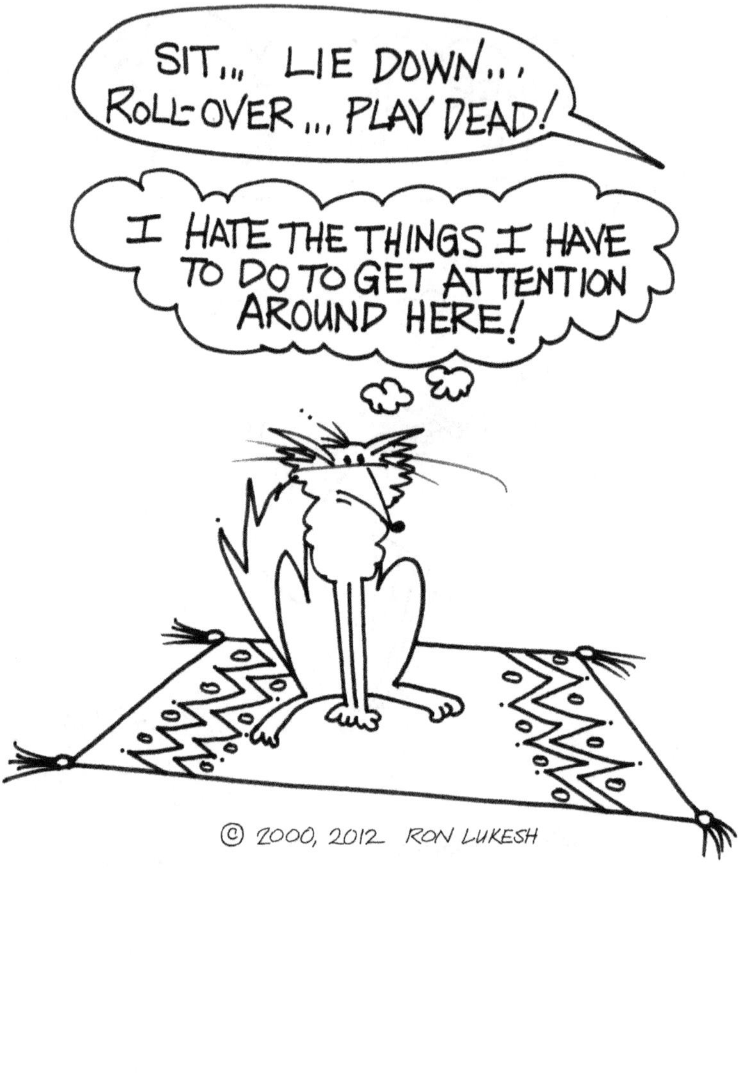
SIT... LIE DOWN...
ROLL-OVER... PLAY DEAD!
I HATE THE THINGS I HAVE TO DO TO GET ATTENTION AROUND HERE!
© 2000, 2012 RON LUKESH

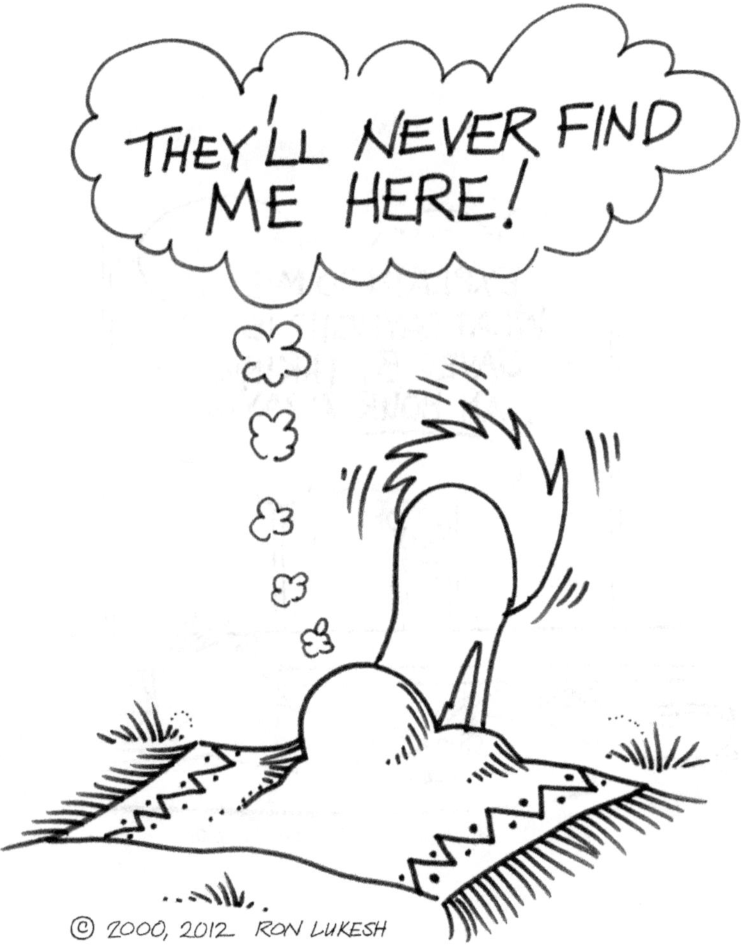
THEY'LL NEVER FIND ME HERE!
© 2000, 2012 RON LUKESH

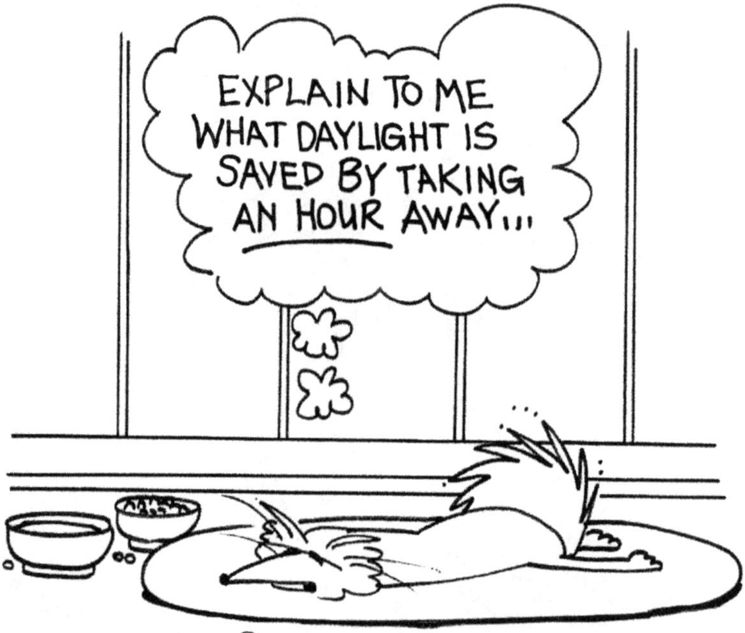
EXPLAIN TO ME WHAT DAYLIGHT IS SAVED BY TAKING AN HOUR AWAY...

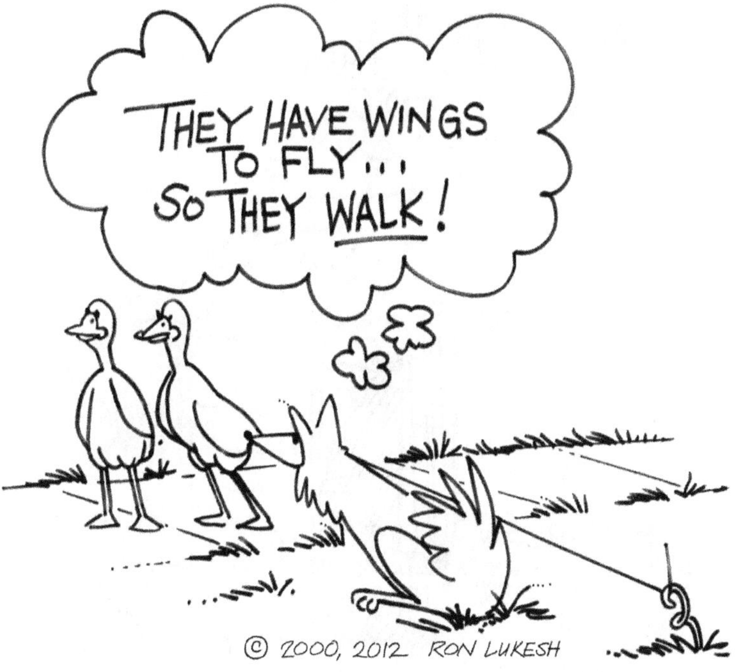
THEY HAVE WINGS TO FLY... SO THEY WALK!
© 2000, 2012 RON LUKESH

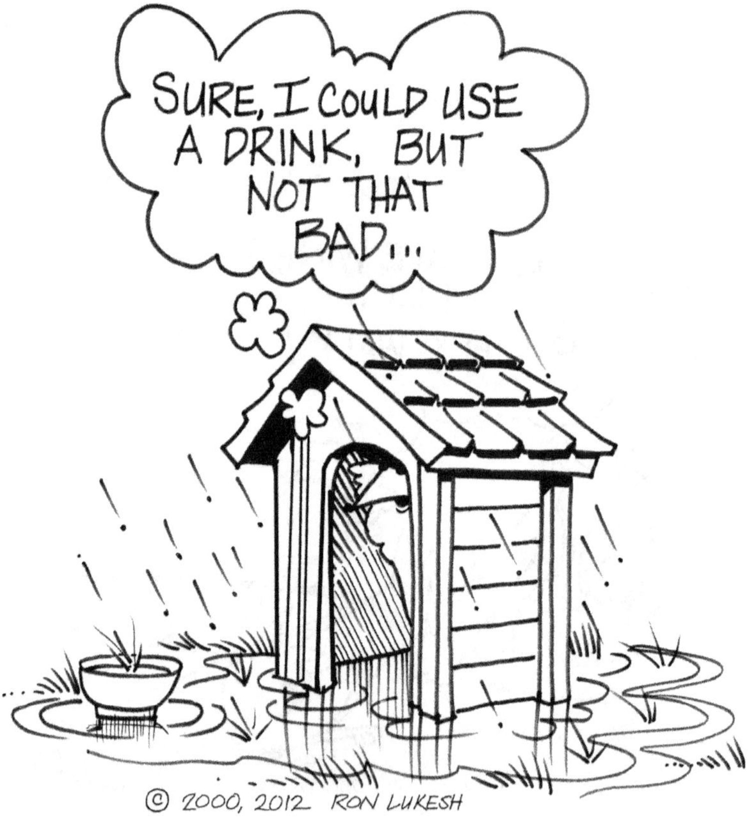
SURE, I COULD USE A DRINK, BUT NOT THAT BAD...
© 2000, 2012 RON LUKESH

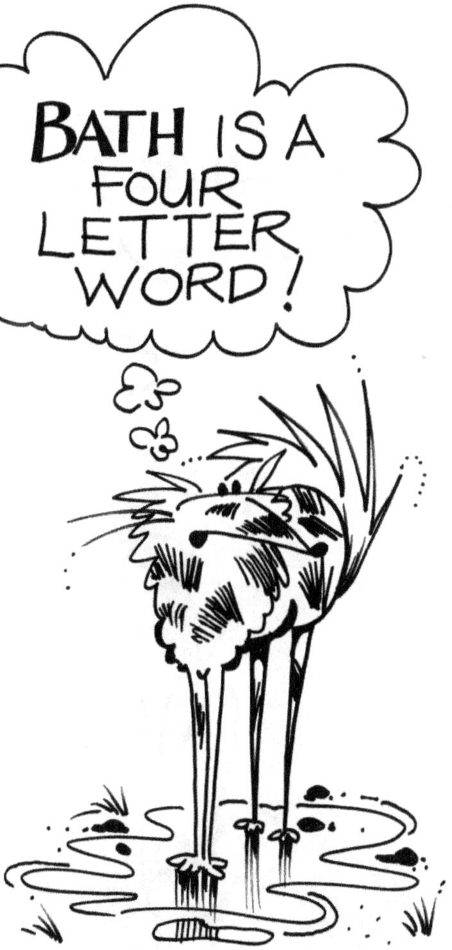
BATH IS A FOUR LETTER WORD!

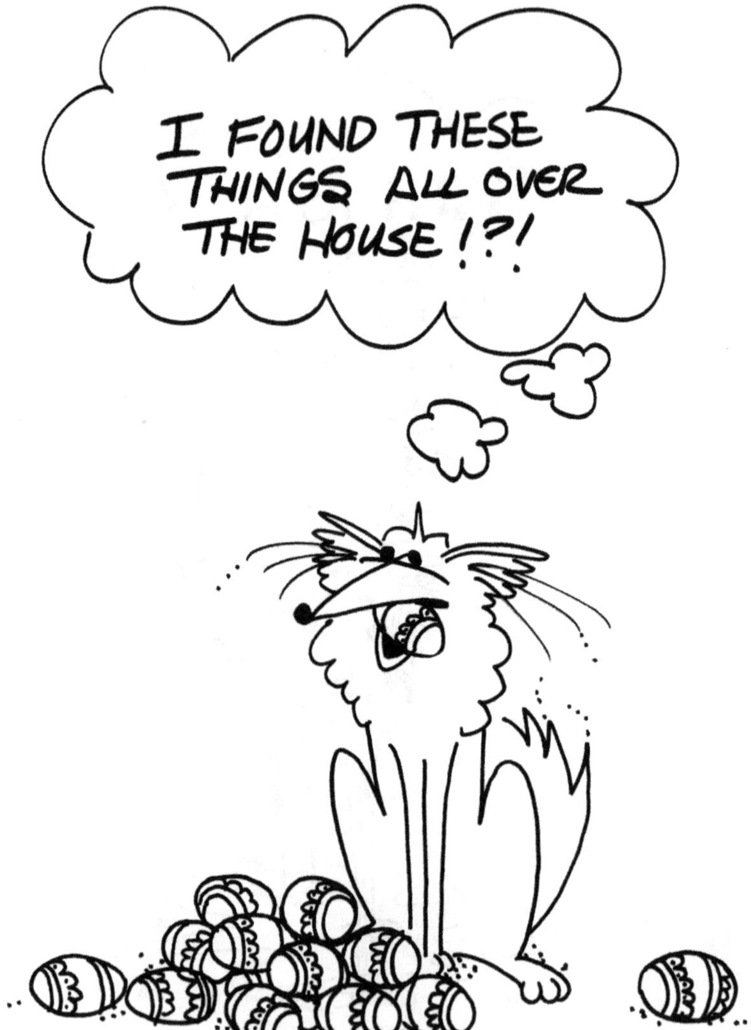
I FOUND THESE THINGS ALL OVER THE HOUSE !?!

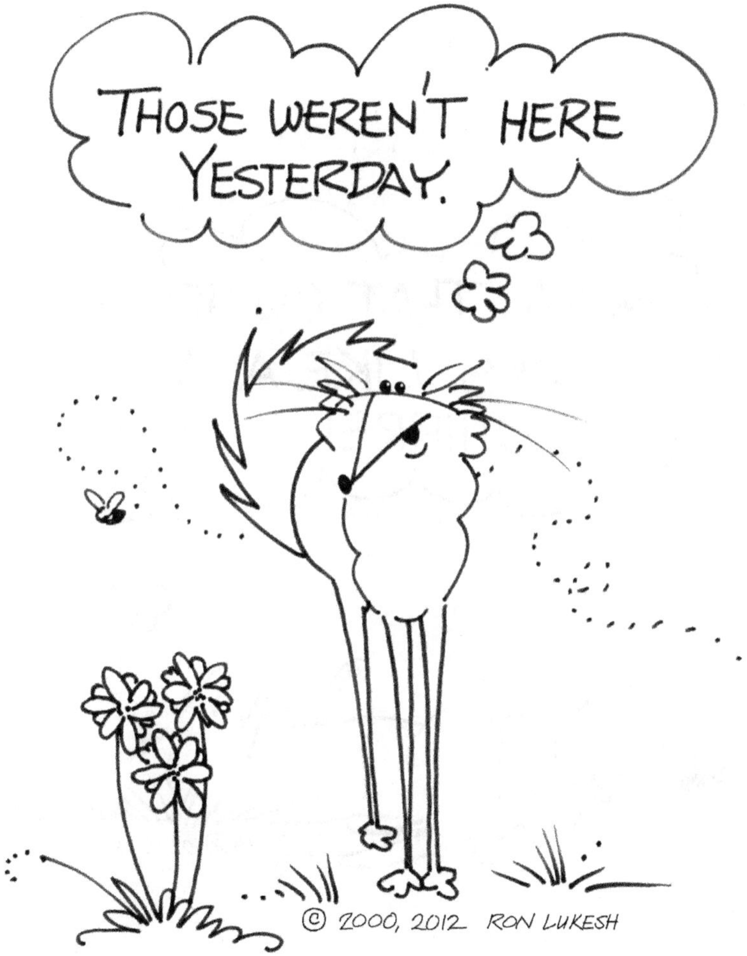
THOSE WEREN'T HERE YESTERDAY.
© 2000, 2012 RON LUKESH

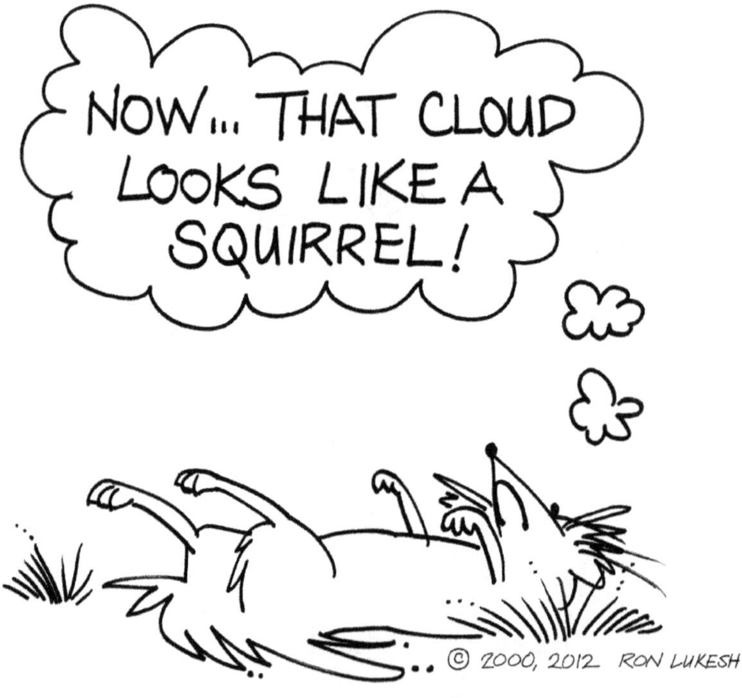
NOW... THAT CLOUD LOOKS LIKE A SQUIRREL!
© 2000, 2012 RON LUKESH

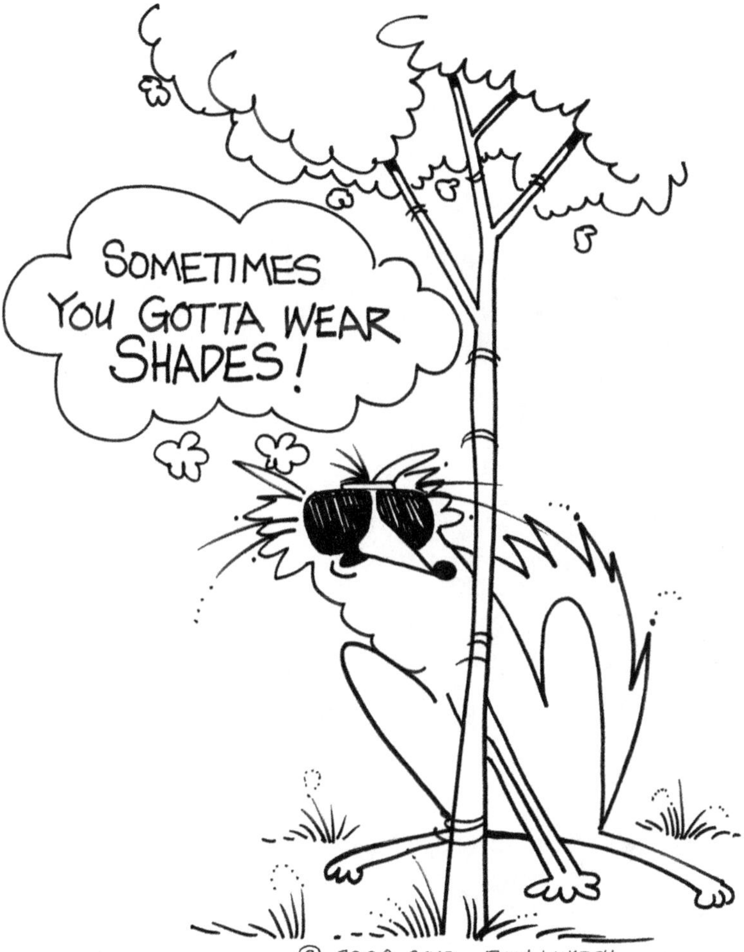
SOMETIMES YOU GOTTA WEAR SHADES!

Summer

© 2000, 2012 RON LUKESH

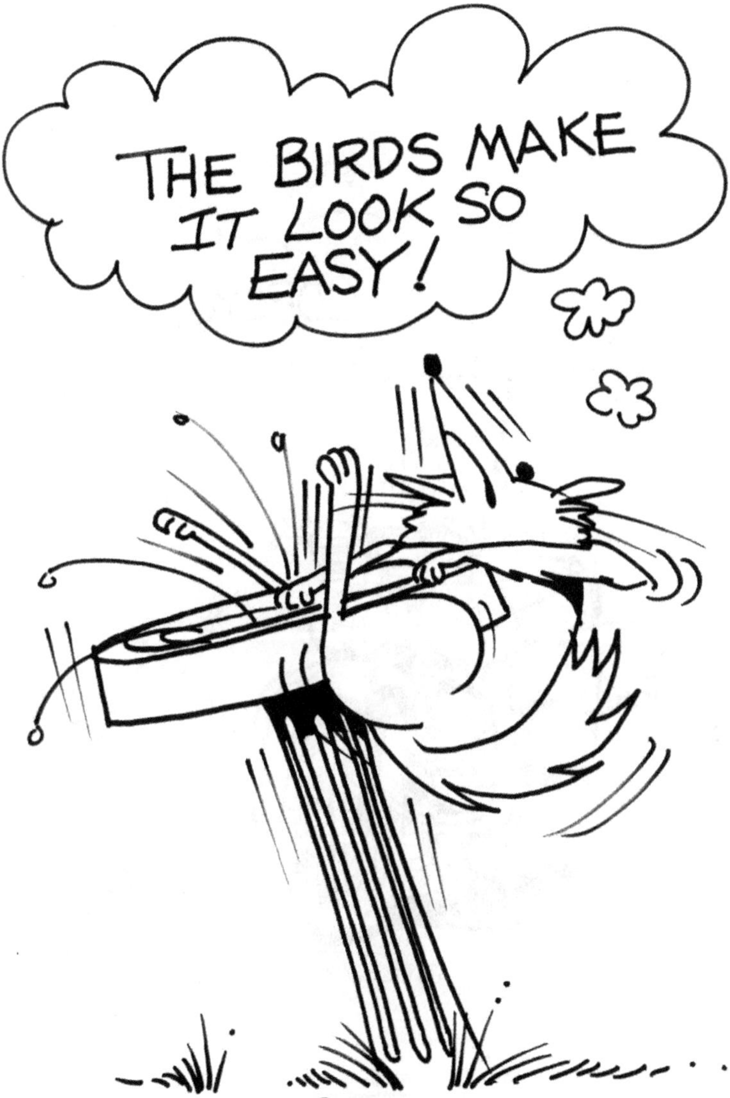
THE BIRDS MAKE IT LOOK SO EASY!
© 2000, 2012 RON LUKESH

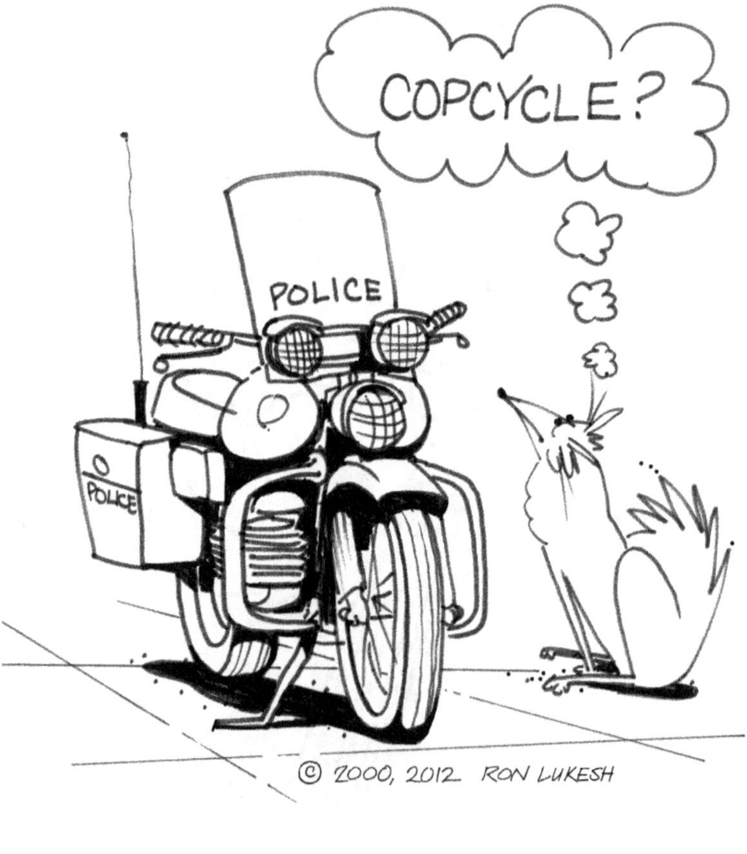
COPCYCLE?
POLICE
POLICE
© 2000, 2012 RON LUKESH

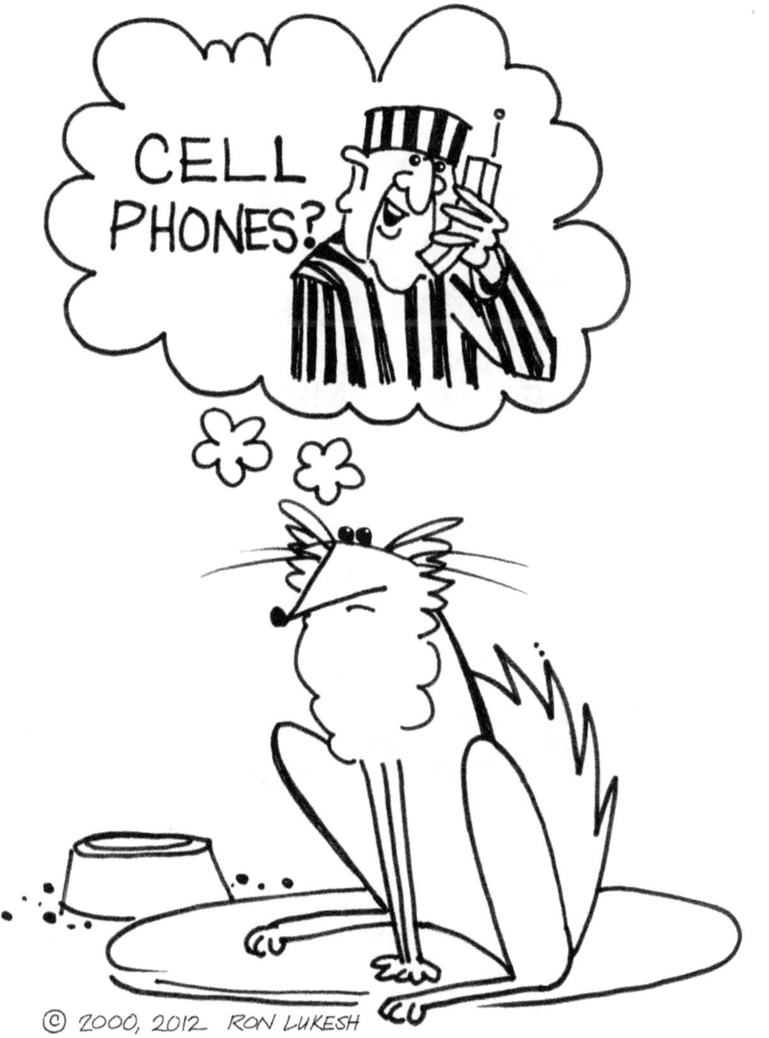
CELL PHONES?

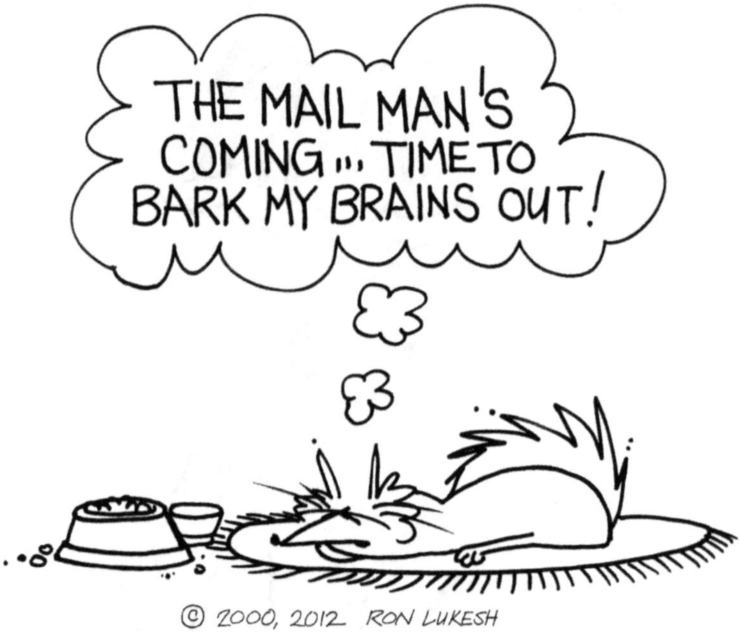
THE MAIL MAN'S COMING... TIME TO BARK MY BRAINS OUT!
© 2000, 2012 RON LUKESH

© 2000, 2012 RON LUKESH

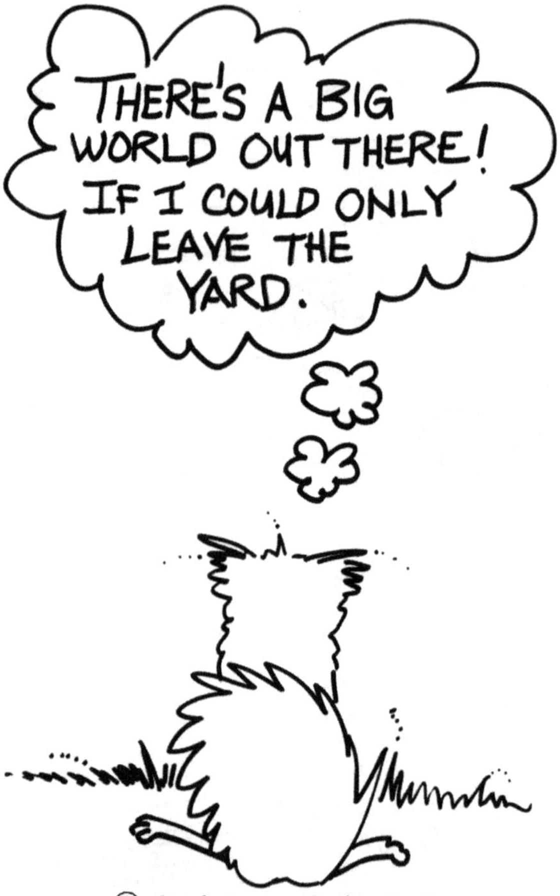
THERE'S A BIG WORLD OUT THERE! IF I COULD ONLY LEAVE THE YARD.

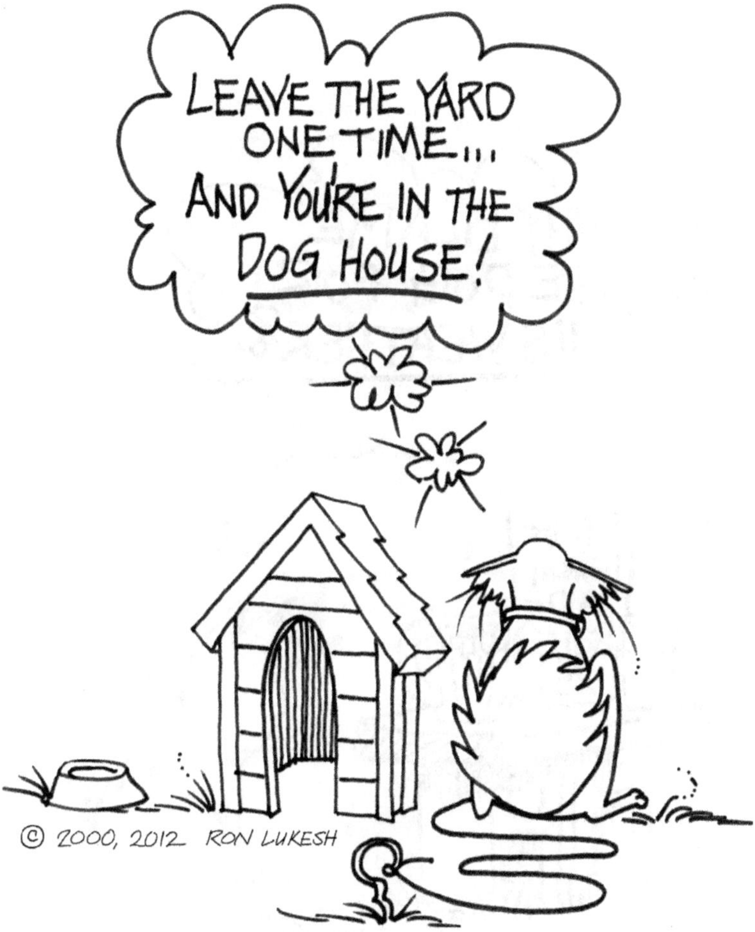
LEAVE THE YARD ONE TIME...
AND YOU'RE IN THE DOG HOUSE!
© 2000, 2012 RON LUKESH

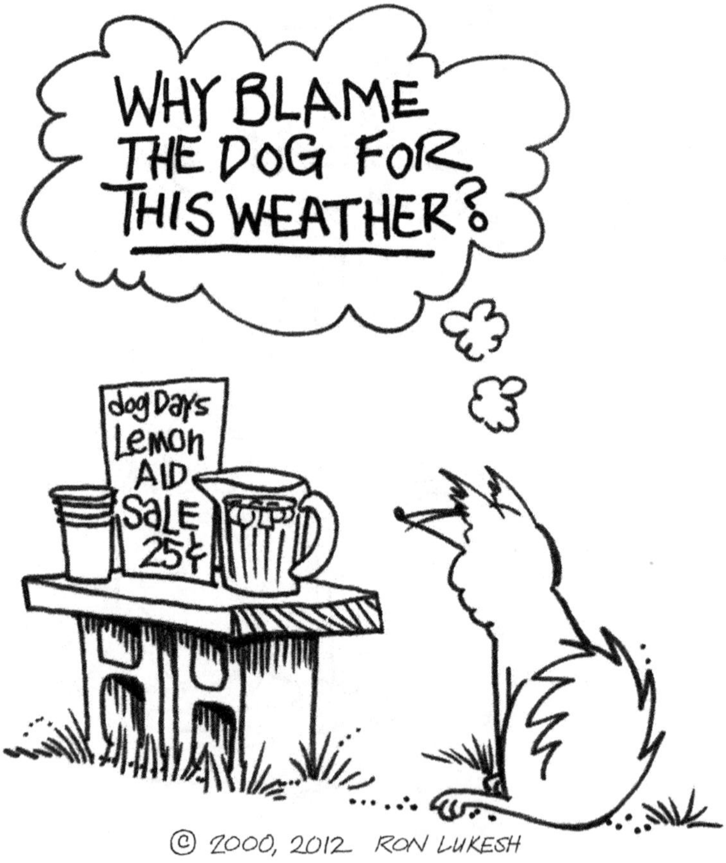
WHY BLAME THE DOG FOR THIS WEATHER?
dog Days Lemon AID SaLE 25¢

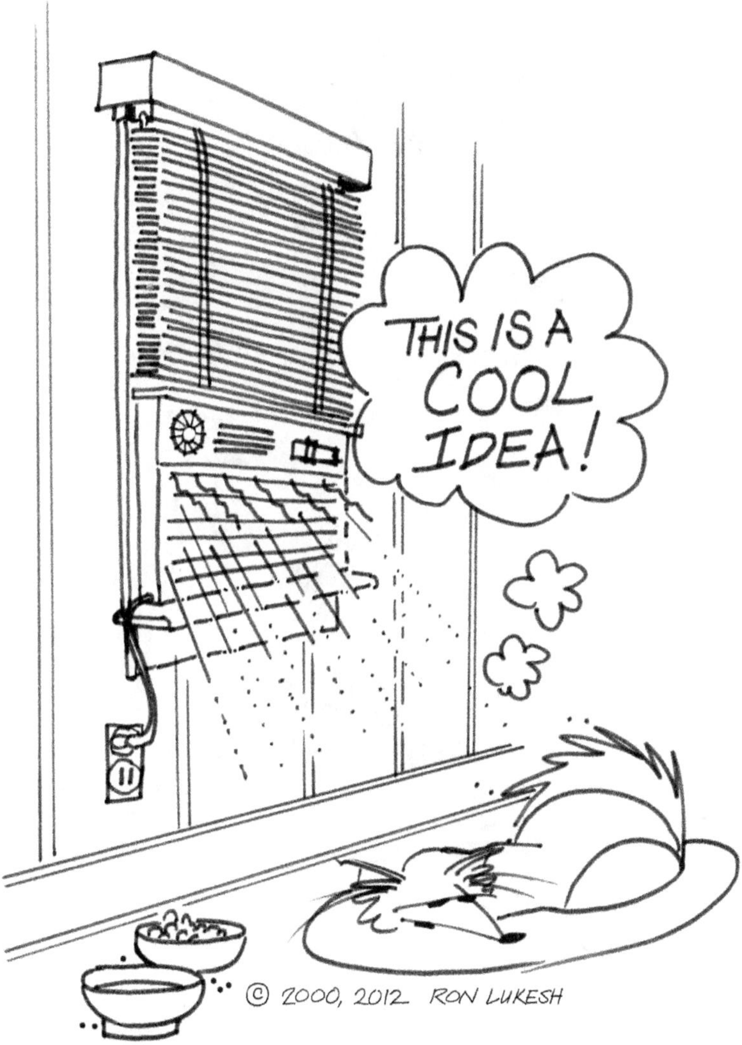
THIS IS A COOL IDEA!

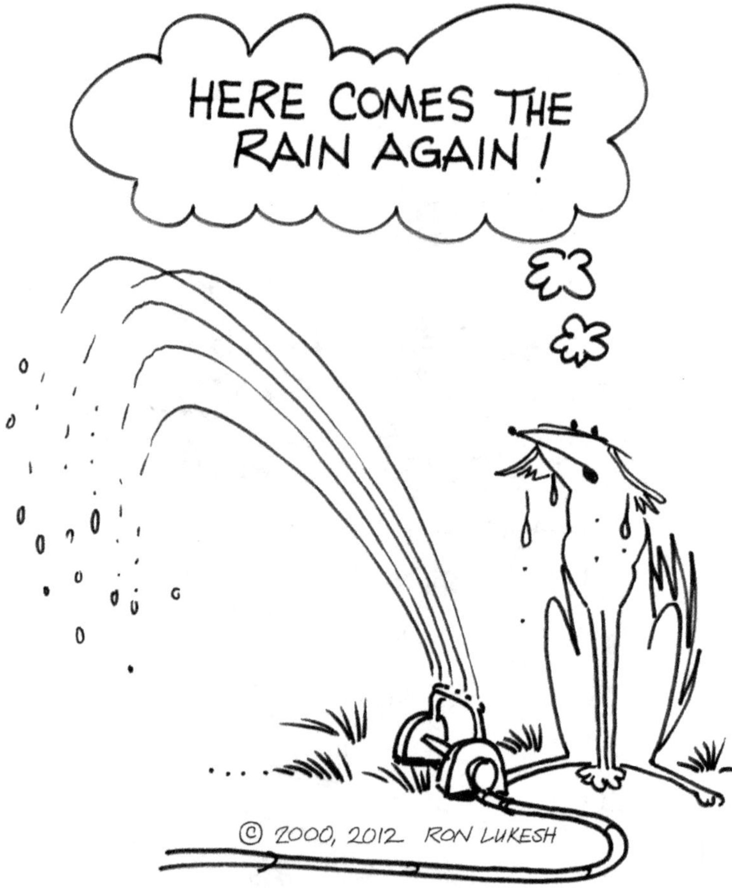
HERE COMES THE RAIN AGAIN!
© 2000, 2012 RON LUKESH

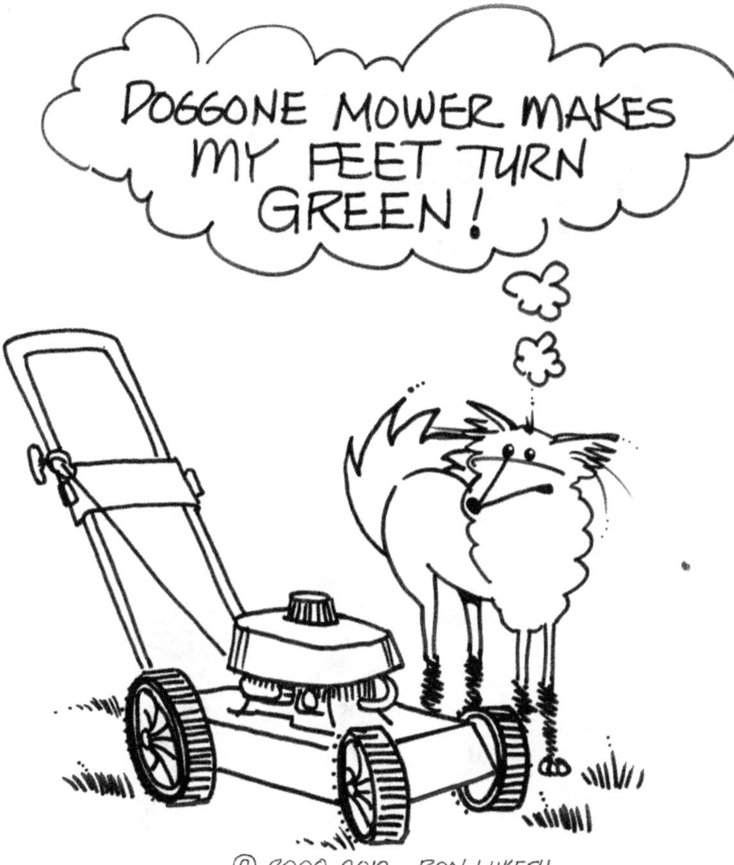
DOGGONE MOWER MAKES MY FEET TURN GREEN!

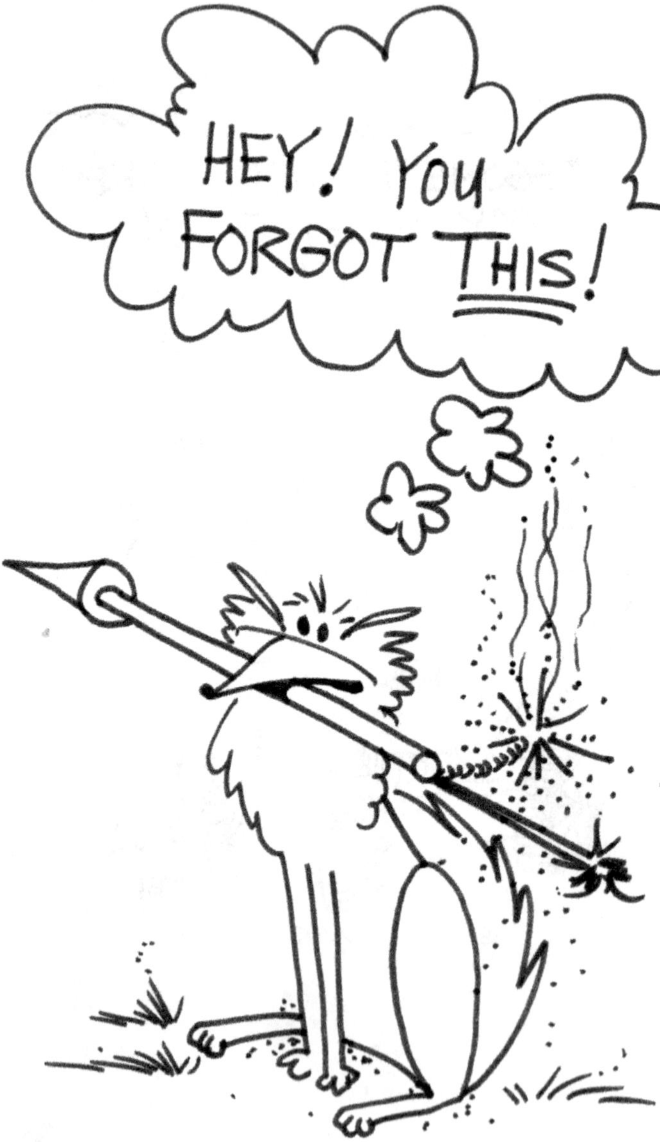
HEY! YOU FORGOT THIS!

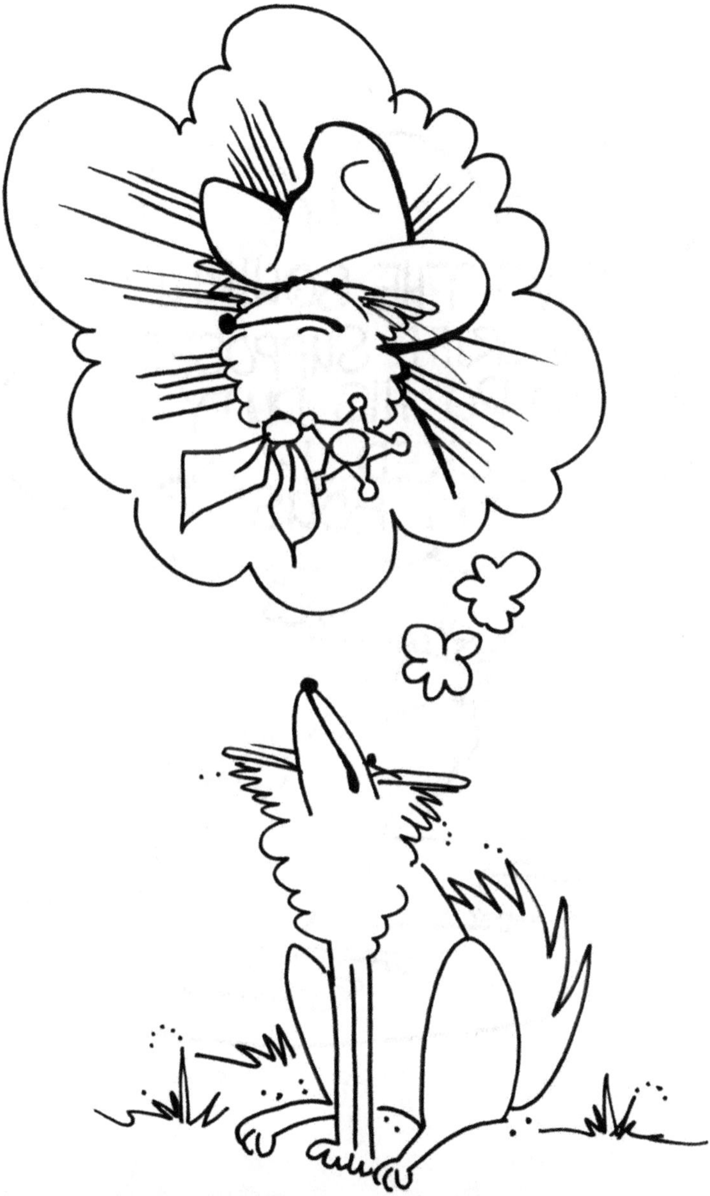

SQUIRREL SHERIFF...

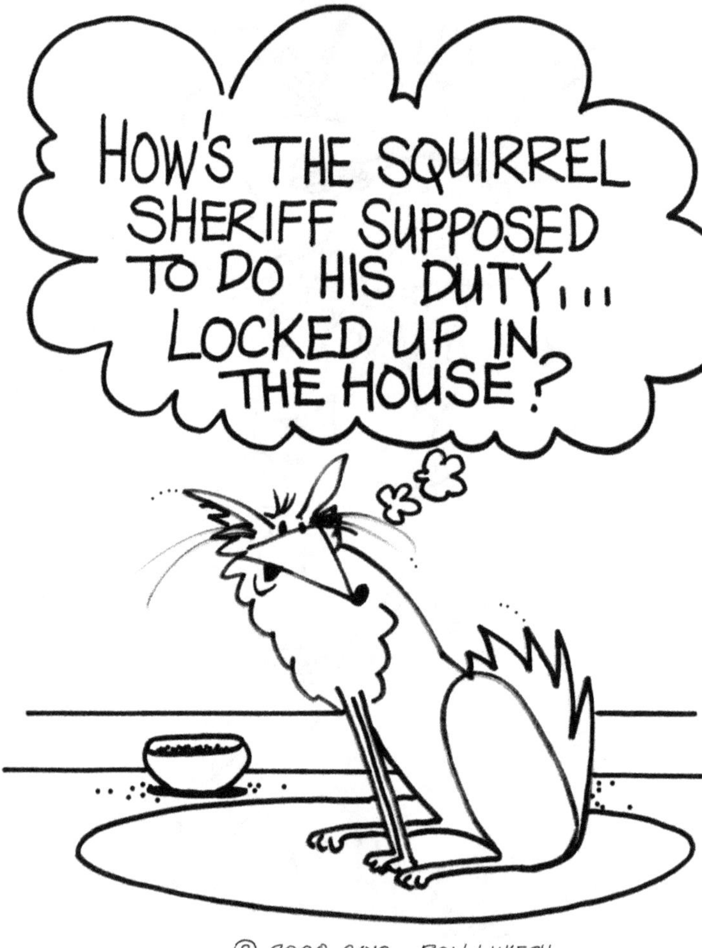
HOW'S THE SQUIRREL SHERIFF SUPPOSED TO DO HIS DUTY... LOCKED UP IN THE HOUSE?

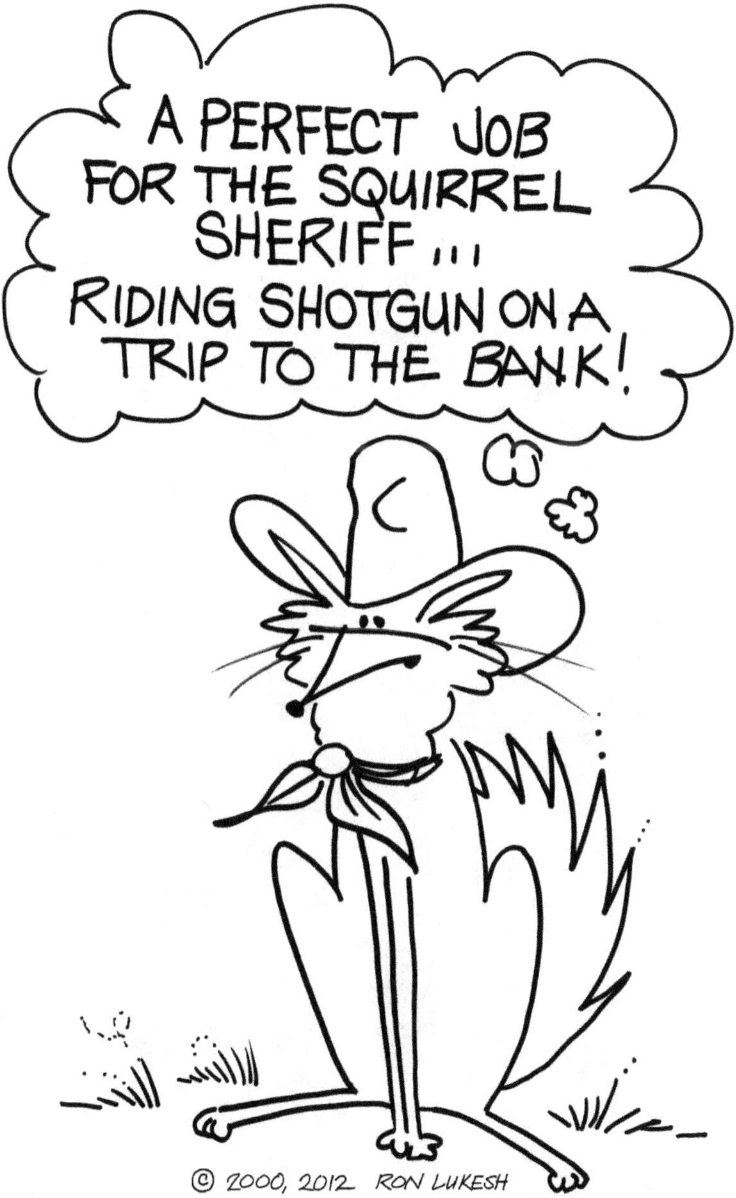
A PERFECT JOB FOR THE SQUIRREL SHERIFF ... RIDING SHOTGUN ON A TRIP TO THE BANK!

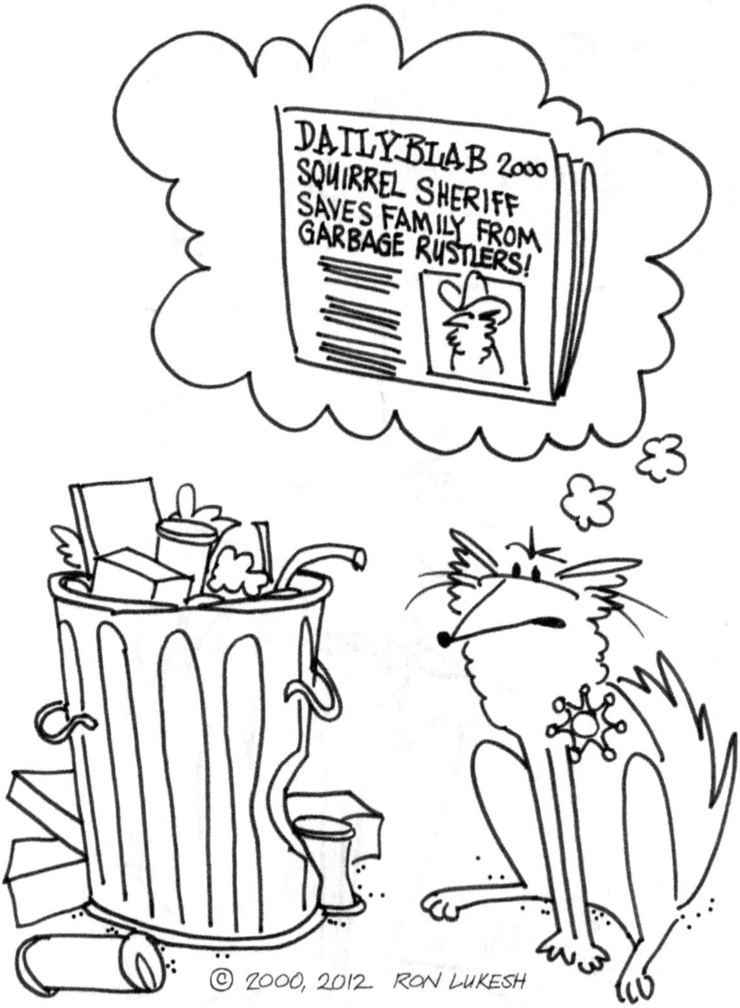
DAILYBLAB 2000
SQUIRREL SHERIFF
SAVES FAMILY FROM
GARBAGE RUSTLERS!

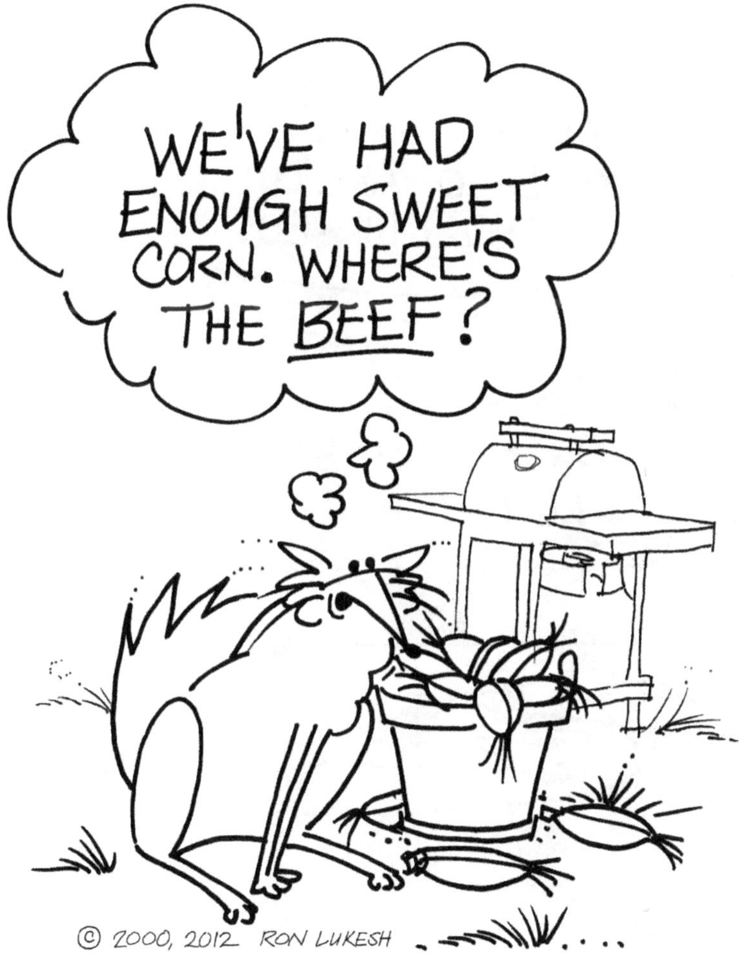
WE'VE HAD ENOUGH SWEET CORN. WHERE'S THE BEEF?
© 2000, 2012 RON LUKESH

HERE'S SOME BREAD TO TAKE OUT TO THE SQUIRRELS!
THAT'S RIGHT... YOU FETCH 'EM... I'LL CATCH 'EM!

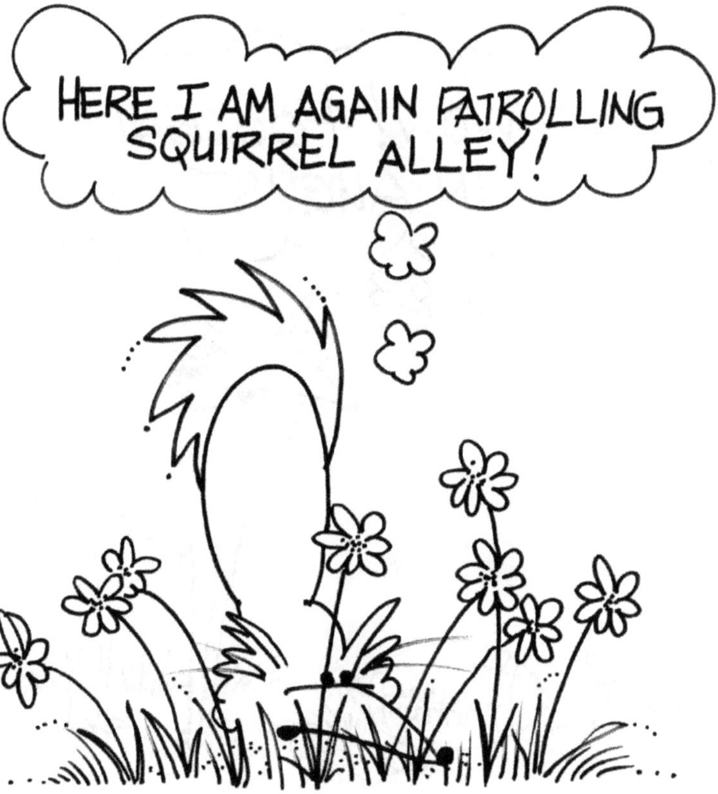
HERE I AM AGAIN PATROLLING SQUIRREL ALLEY!

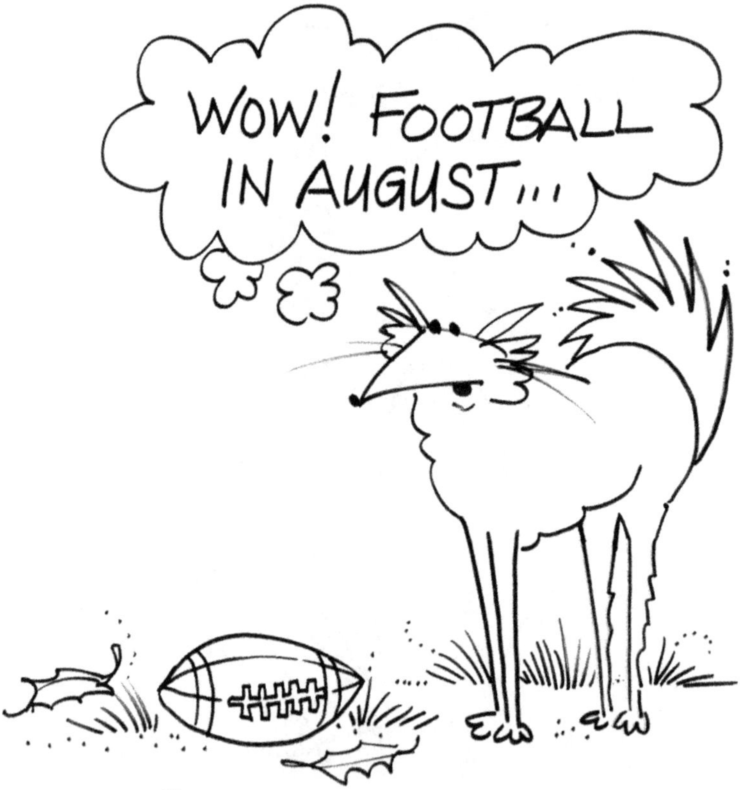
WOW! FOOTBALL IN AUGUST...

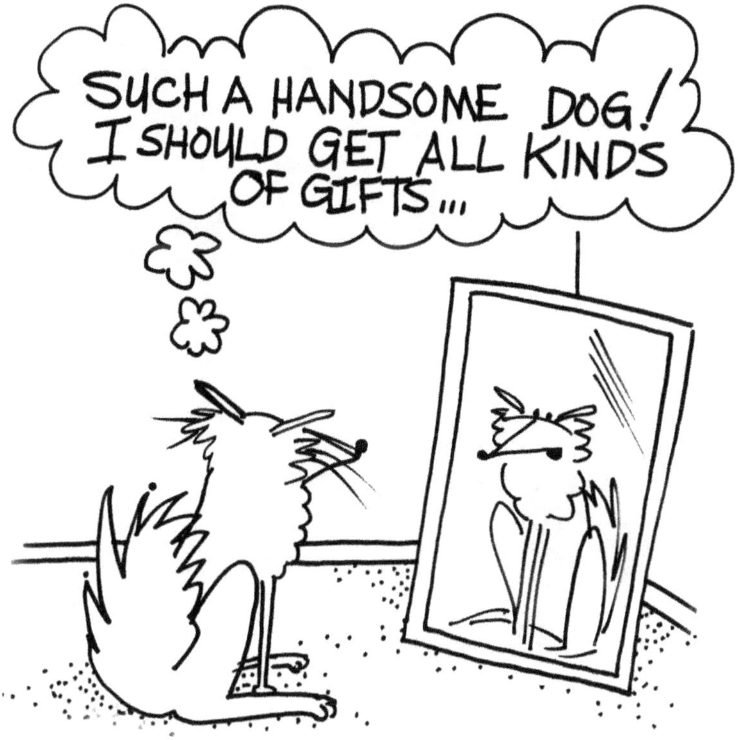
SUCH A HANDSOME DOG! I SHOULD GET ALL KINDS OF GIFTS...

NATIONAL DOG DAY...

Fall

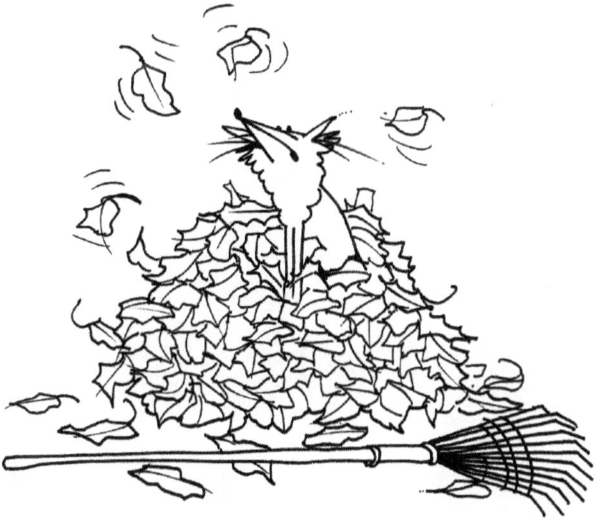

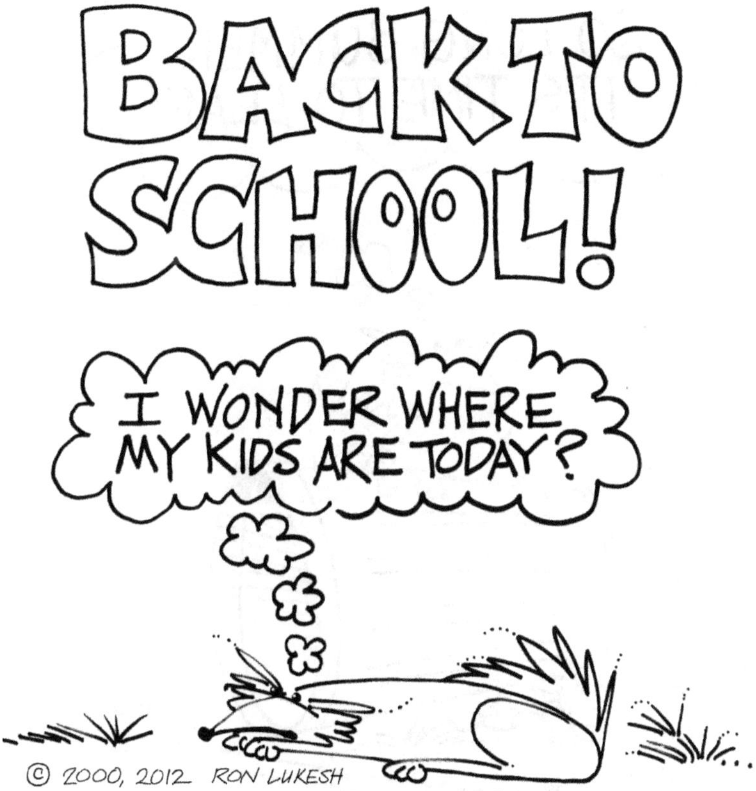
BACK TO SCHOOL!
I WONDER WHERE MY KIDS ARE TODAY?
© 2000, 2012 RON LUKESH

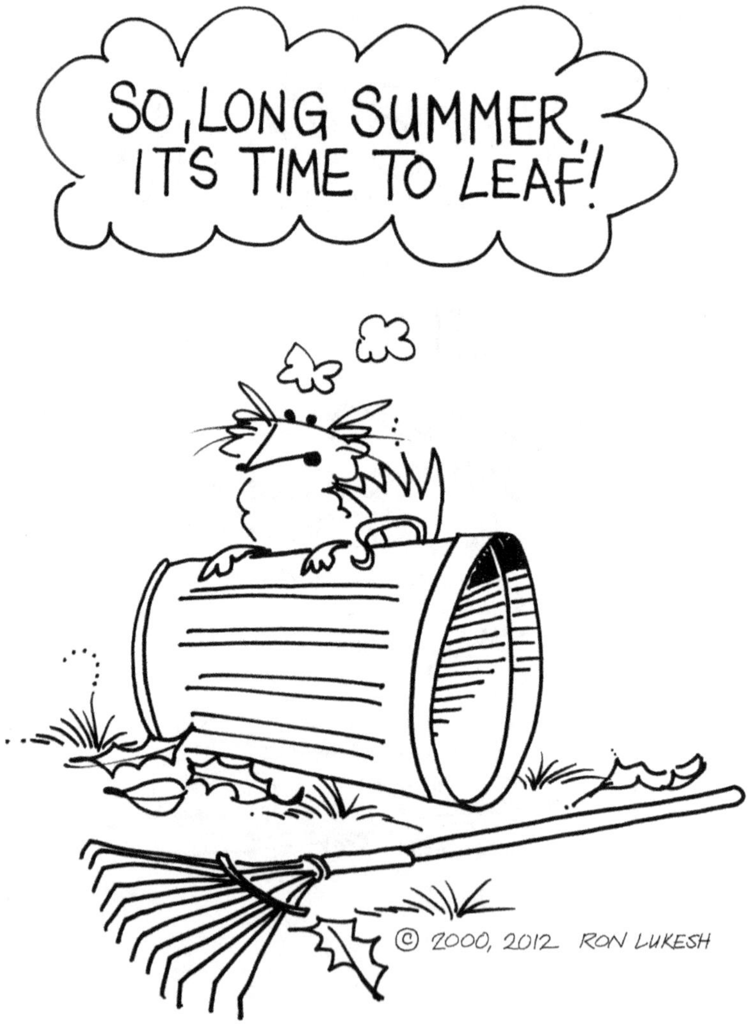
SO, LONG SUMMER, IT'S TIME TO LEAF!
© 2000, 2012 RON LUKESH

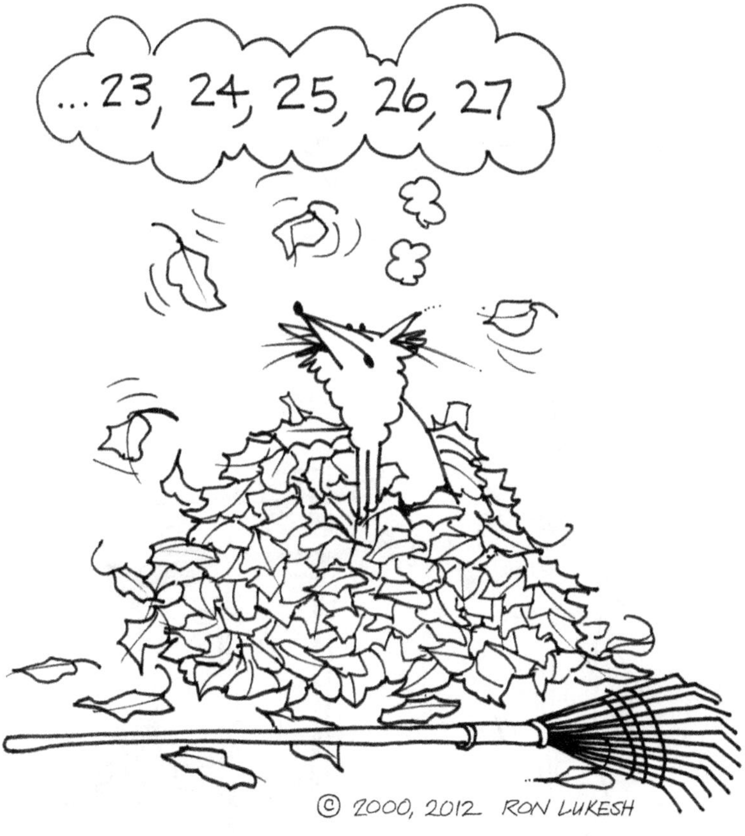
...23, 24, 25, 26, 27
© 2000, 2012 RON LUKESH

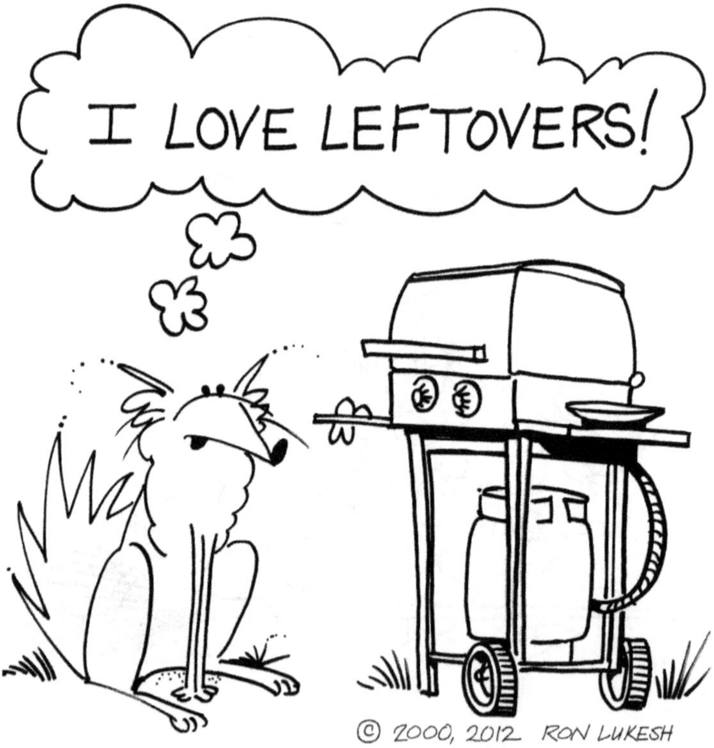
I LOVE LEFTOVERS!
© 2000, 2012 RON LUKESH

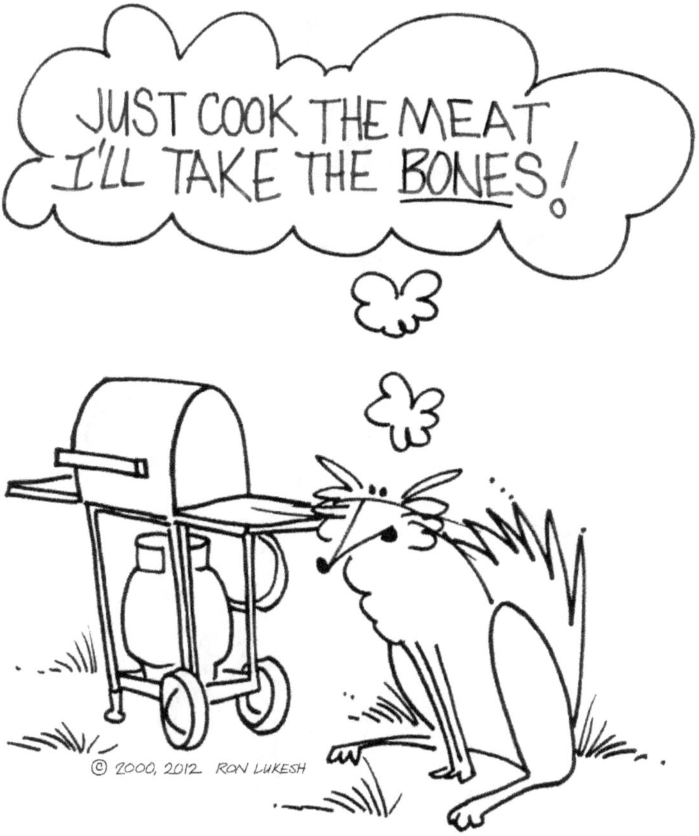
JUST COOK THE MEAT
I'LL TAKE THE BONES!
© 2000, 2012 RON LUKESH

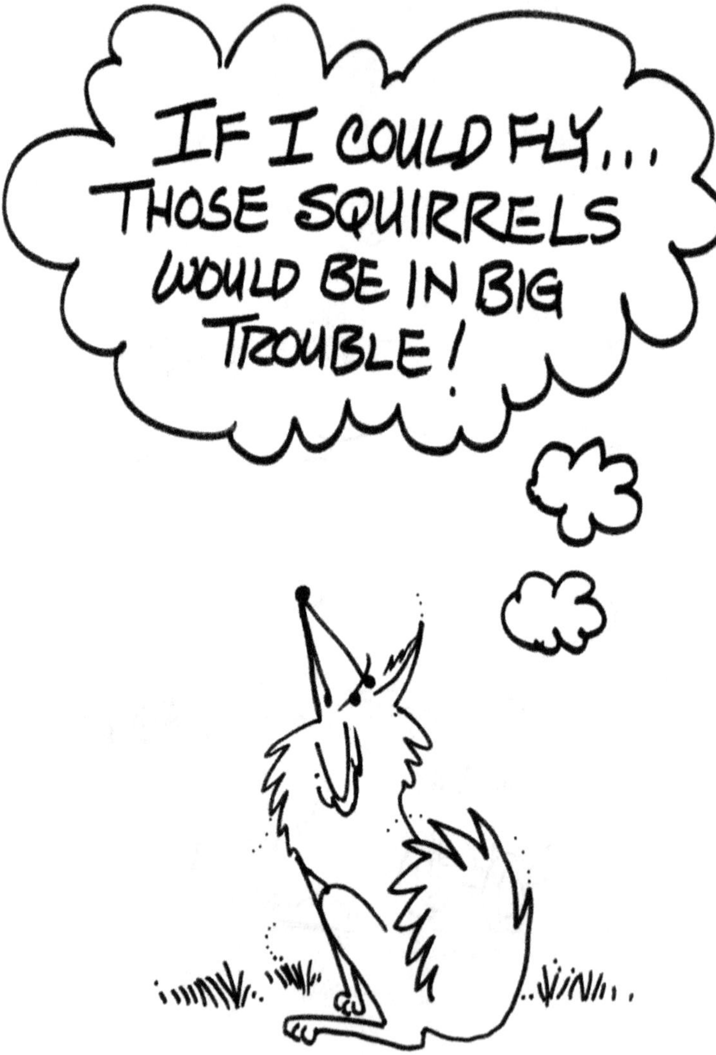
IF I COULD FLY...
THOSE SQUIRRELS
WOULD BE IN BIG
TROUBLE!

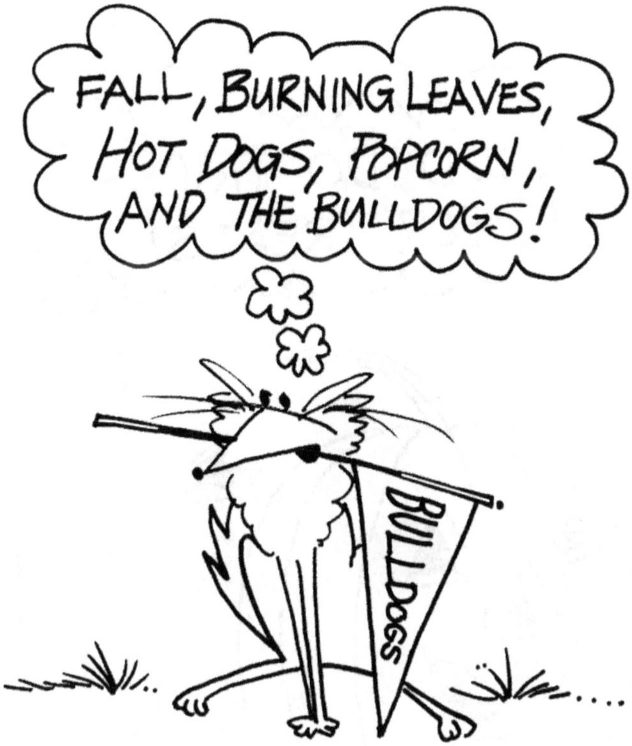
FALL, BURNING LEAVES,
HOT DOGS, POPCORN,
AND THE BULLDOGS!
BULLDOGS

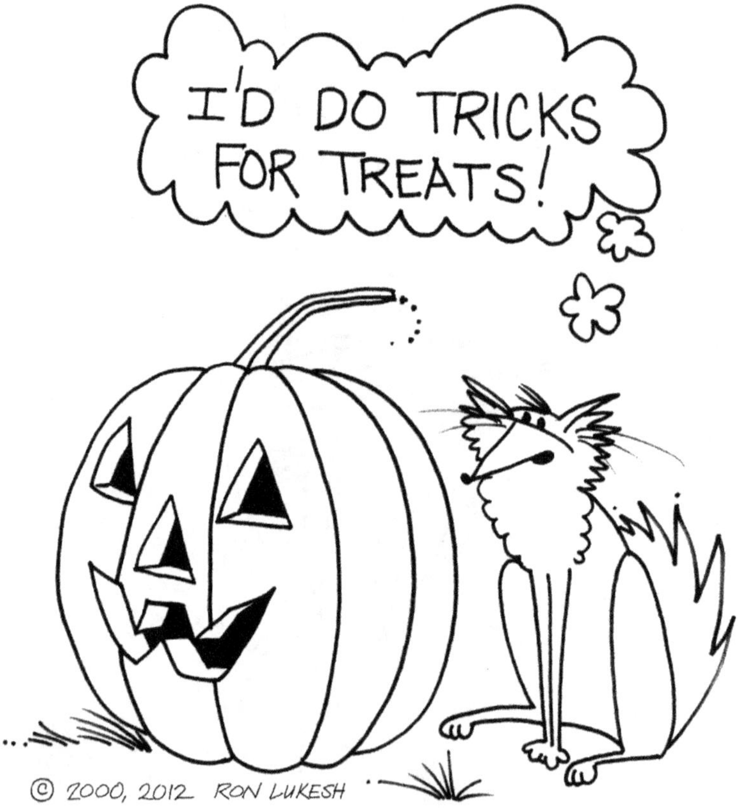
I'D DO TRICKS FOR TREATS!
© 2000, 2012 RON LUKESH

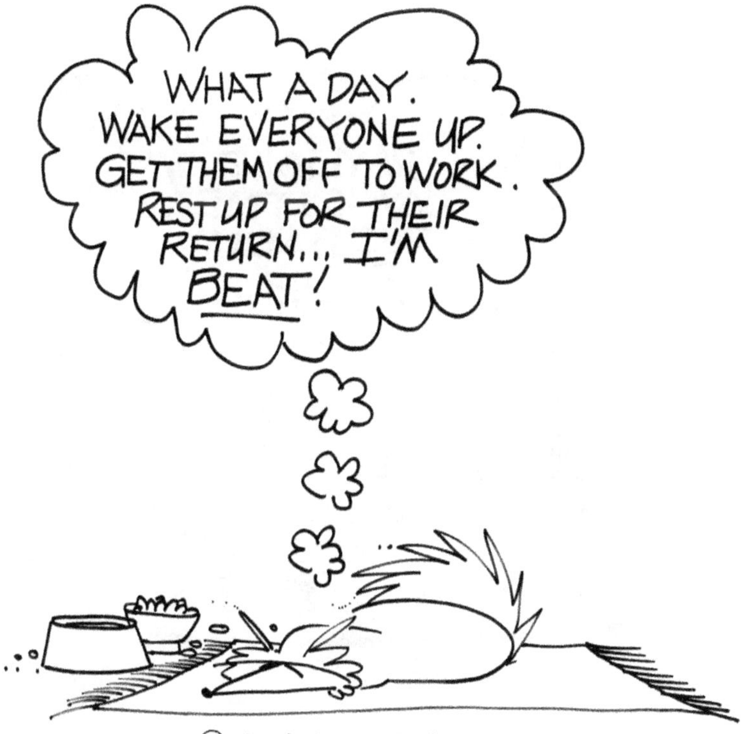
WHAT A DAY.
WAKE EVERYONE UP.
GET THEM OFF TO WORK.
REST UP FOR THEIR RETURN... I'M BEAT!

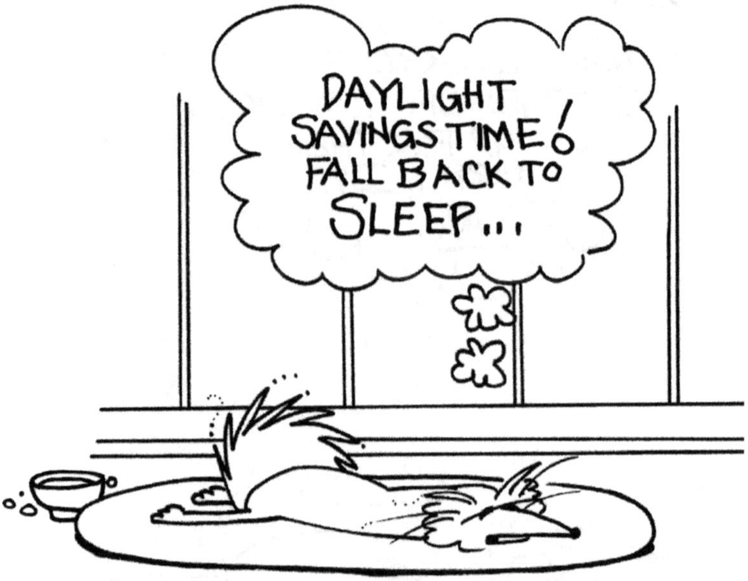
DAYLIGHT SAVINGS TIME!
FALL BACK TO SLEEP...

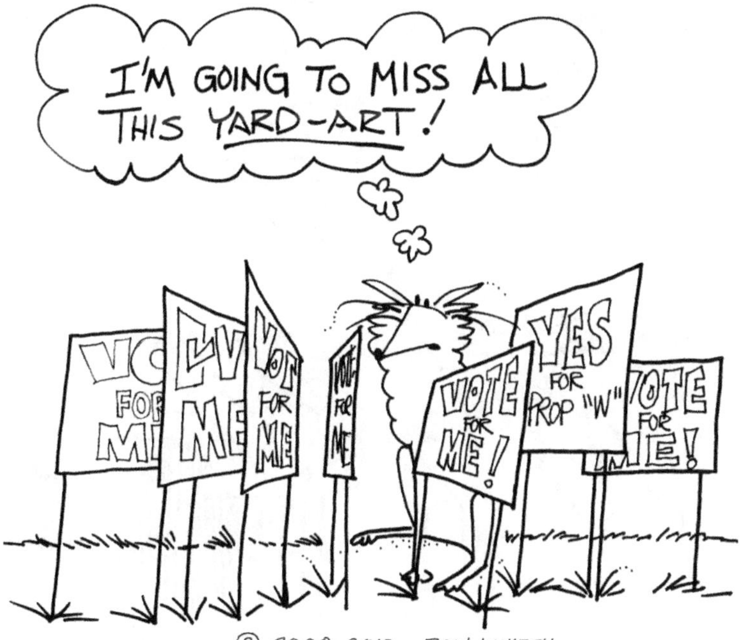
I'M GOING TO MISS ALL THIS YARD-ART!
VOTE FOR ME
VOTE FOR ME
VOTE FOR ME
VOTE FOR ME
VOTE FOR ME!
YES FOR PROP "W"
VOTE FOR ME!

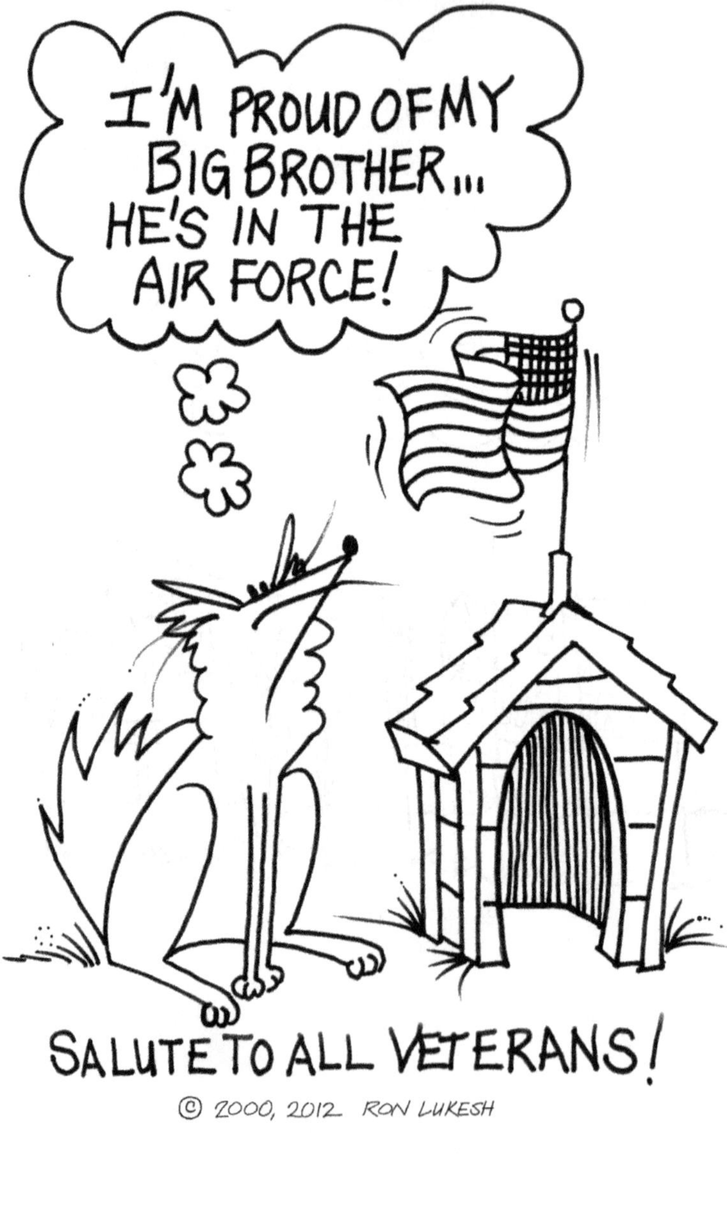
I'M PROUD OF MY BIG BROTHER... HE'S IN THE AIR FORCE!

SALUTE TO ALL VETERANS!

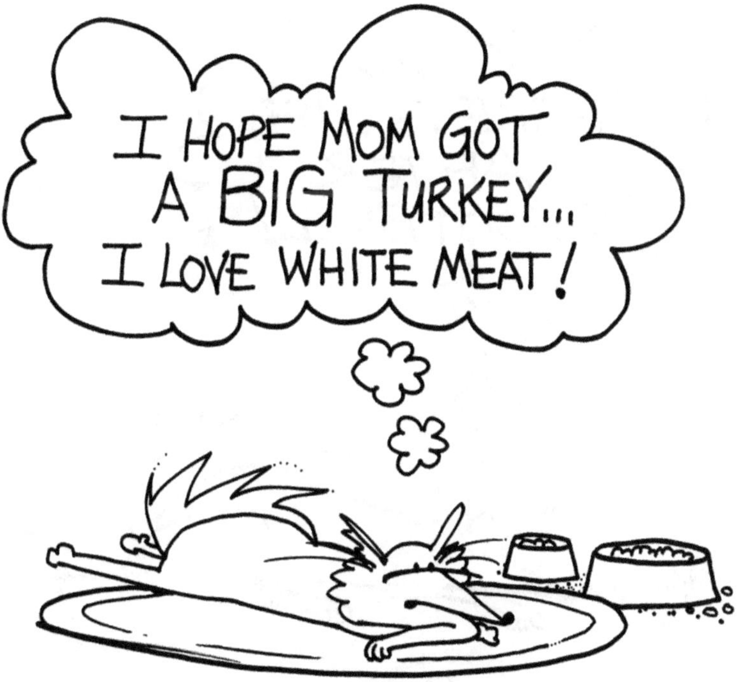
I HOPE MOM GOT
A BIG TURKEY...
I LOVE WHITE MEAT!

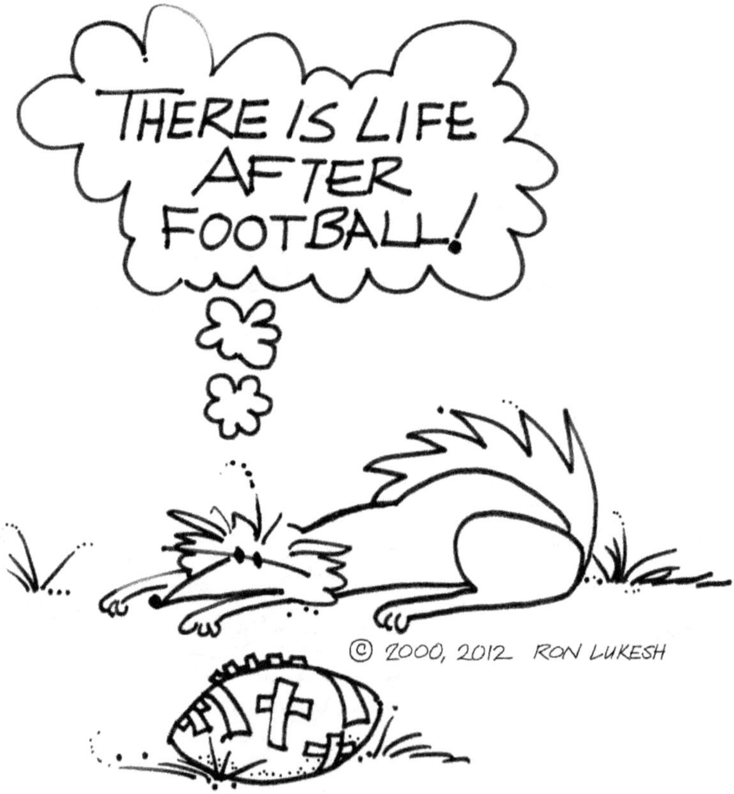
THERE IS LIFE AFTER FOOTBALL!
© 2000, 2012 RON LUKESH

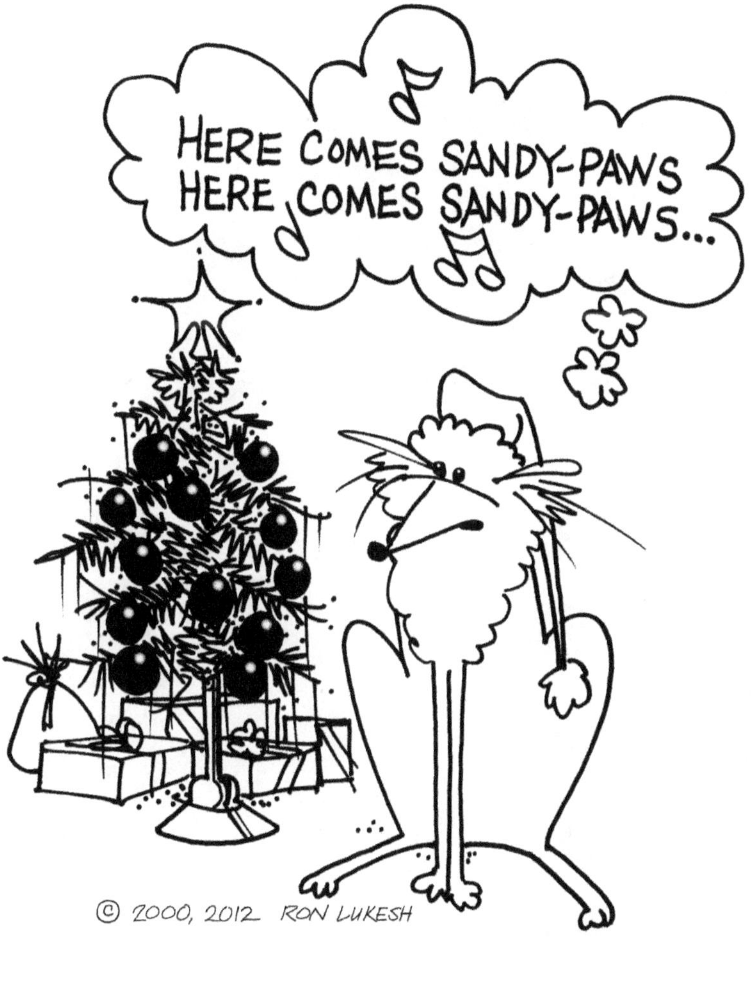
HERE COMES SANDY-PAWS
HERE COMES SANDY-PAWS...

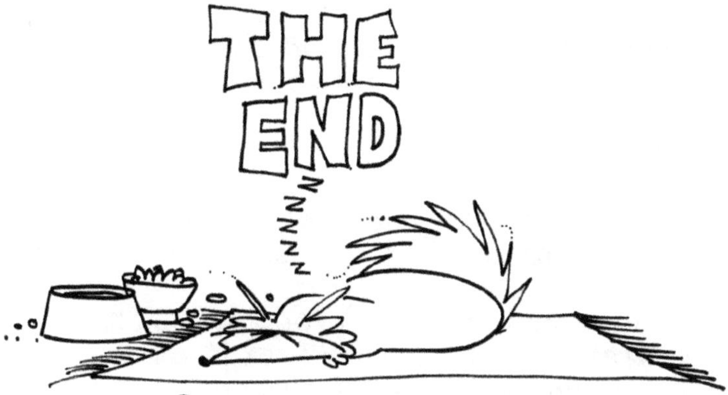
THE END

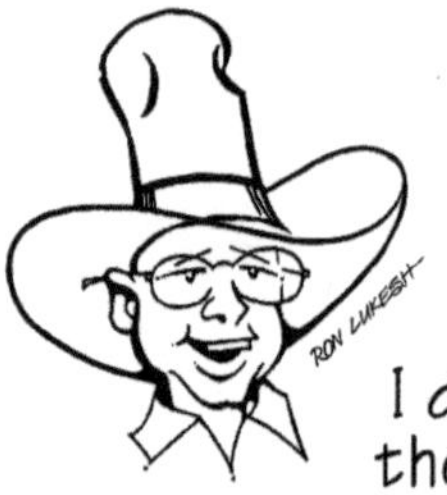
RON LUKESH

My name is Ron Lukesh and
I'M AN ART-A-HOLIC!

My friends say...
"You're all hat and no cattle."
They're right, but I've got horses!

I did my first published artwork at the age of 12. I've never stopped doing artwork. I love what I do.

You name it... I've done it! Over 500 Business Logo Designs, and production art to implement them. I've designed and produced Outdoor Signage, Custom Building Rehabilitations, Paint Schemes for Airlines, and decals for Police Cruisers even Busses.

I actually designed a microwave popcorn bag and packaging for industrial tools. It's all packaging.

I pride myself on Book Cover Designs and Illustrations. But my very first love is cartooning. Heck, that's me up top... and to show you I can draw, that's me down there too!

Actually I believe like some Native Americans do. I'm afraid that the camera will steal my soul. Good luck finding a picture of me, but those who know me would say that's me down here, some 53 years out of my first art job, and it won't be my last if I can help it!

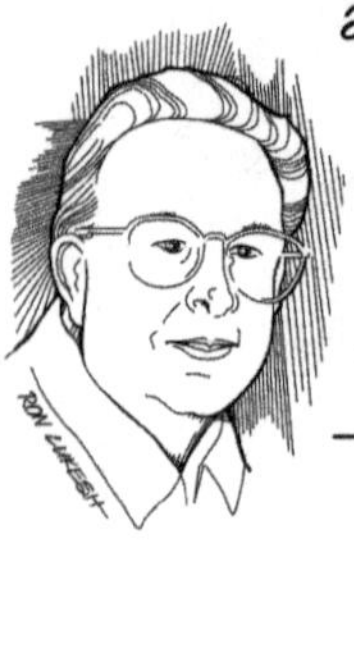
RON LUKESH

I hope you enjoy BO DOG, like we did. A man's measured by the way he treats his animals. "So treat them right and you've got a friend for life."

—————————— Ron

Available at bookstores, online bookstores, and www.fieldmousebooks.com or www.fieldmouseproductions.com

www.ingramcontent.com/pod-product-compliance
Lightning Source LLC
Chambersburg PA
CBHW071737040426
42446CB00012B/2389